FIGHTING FOR THEIR COUNTRY: MINORITIES AT WAR

Minority Soldiers Fighting in the American Revolution

ERIC REEDER

Cavendish Square
New York

Published in 2018 by Cavendish Square Publishing, LLC
243 5th Avenue, Suite 136, New York, NY 10016

Copyright © 2018 by Cavendish Square Publishing, LLC

First Edition

No part of this publication may be reproduced, stored in a retrieval system, or transmitted in any form or by any means—electronic, mechanical, photocopying, recording, or otherwise—without the prior permission of the copyright owner. Request for permission should be addressed to Permissions, Cavendish Square Publishing, 243 5th Avenue, Suite 136, New York, NY 10016. Tel (877) 980-4450; fax (877) 980-4454.

Website: cavendishsq.com

This publication represents the opinions and views of the author based on his or her personal experience, knowledge, and research. The information in this book serves as a general guide only. The author and publisher have used their best efforts in preparing this book and disclaim liability rising directly or indirectly from the use and application of this book.

CPSIA Compliance Information: Batch #CS17CSQ

All websites were available and accurate when this book was sent to press.

Library of Congress Cataloging-in-Publication Data

Names: Reeder, Eric.
Title: Minority soldiers fighting in the American Revolution / Eric Reeder.
Description: New York : Cavendish Square, 2018. | Series: Fighting for their country: minorities at war | Includes index.
Identifiers: ISBN 9781502626615 (library bound) | ISBN 9781502626554 (ebook)
Subjects: LCSH: United States--History--Revolution, 1775-1783--Juvenile literature. | United States--History--Revolution, 1775-1783--African Americans--Juvenile literature. | Indians of North America--History--Revolution, 1775-1783--Juvenile literature.
Classification: LCC E208.R44 2018 | DDC 973.3--dc23

Editorial Director: David McNamara
Editor: Caitlyn Miller
Copy Editor: Alex Tessman
Associate Art Director: Amy Greenan
Designer: Stephanie Flecha
Production Coordinator: Karol Szymczuk
Photo Research: J8 Media

The photographs in this book are used by permission and through the courtesy of:
Cover Superstock/Getty Images; p. 4 World Digital Library/Wikimedia Commons/ File:Soldiers in Uniform WDL2960.png/Public Domain; p. 10 Library of Congress/Corbis Historical/Getty Images; p. 14 Wellcome Library, London/Wikimedia Commons/File:John Wesley preaching to native American Indians. Engraving. Wellcome V0006867.jpg/CC BY 4.0; p. 16, 28, 41 MPI/Getty Images; p. 20 Victorian Traditions/Shutterstock.com; p. 21, 96 Stock Montage/Getty Images; p. 25 Henry Alexander Ogden/Wikimedia Commons/File:The Victory of Montcalms Troops at Carillon by Henry Alexander Ogden.JPG/Public Domain; p. 26 Historical poetical and pictorial American scenes by J.W. Barber, 1850/Wikimedia Commons/File:Benezet.jpg/Public Domain; p. 35 The Print Collector/Hulton Archive/Getty Images; p. 38 Universal History Archive/Getty Images; p. 43 John Trumbull/Wikimedia Commons/ File:Surrender of Lord Cornwallis (cropped).jpg/Public Domain; p. 46 Joshua Reynolds/Google Cultural Institute/ Wikimedia Commons/File:Sir Joshua Reynolds - John Murray, 4th Earl of Dunmore - Google Art Project.jpg/Public Domain; p. 47 John Murray, 4th Earl Dunmore/LOC/Wikimedia Commons/File:DunmoresProclamation.jpg/Public Domain; p. 51 Smith Collection/Gado/Getty Images; p. 54, 77 Library of Congress; p. 56 The Valentine; p. 59 Everett Historical/Shutterstock.com; p. 64 Imagno/Getty Images; p. 66 NYPL/Wikimedia Commons/File:The brave old Hendrick, the great Sachem or chief of the Mohawk Indians, one of the six nations now in alliance with, and subject to the king of Great Britain (NYPL NYPG94-F42-419784).jpg/Public Domain; p. 72 M'r Michel Capitaine du Chesnoy, A.d.C. du Général LaFayette/LOC/Wikimedia Commons/File:Barren-hill-map.jpg/Public Domain; p. 73 John Reuben Chapin/ Wikimedia Commons/File:Battle of Oriskany.jpg/Public Domain; p. 80 Randy Duchaine/Alamy Stock Photo; p. 82 Time Life Pictures/Mansell/The LIFE Picture Collection/Getty Images; p. 86 Howard Chandler Christy/Wikimedia Commons/ File:Scene at the Signing of the Constitution of the United States.jpg/Public Domain; p. 88 Francis G. Mayer/Corbis/ VCG via Getty Images; p. 95 George Ostertag/Alamy Stock Photo; p. 98 PRISMA ARCHIVO/Alamy Stock Photo.

Printed in the United States of America

CONTENTS

INTRODUCTION:
The Minorities Who Fought
in the Revolutionary War 5

1 Life at Home. 11

2 The Revolutionary War Itself. 29

3 A Waiter Spying
 on the British: A Case Study. 51

4 Oneida and Tuscarora
 Indians in the War: A Case Study. 67

5 A Hero's Welcome?. 81

Glossary. 100

Bibliography 103

Further Information 106

Index 108

About the Author 112

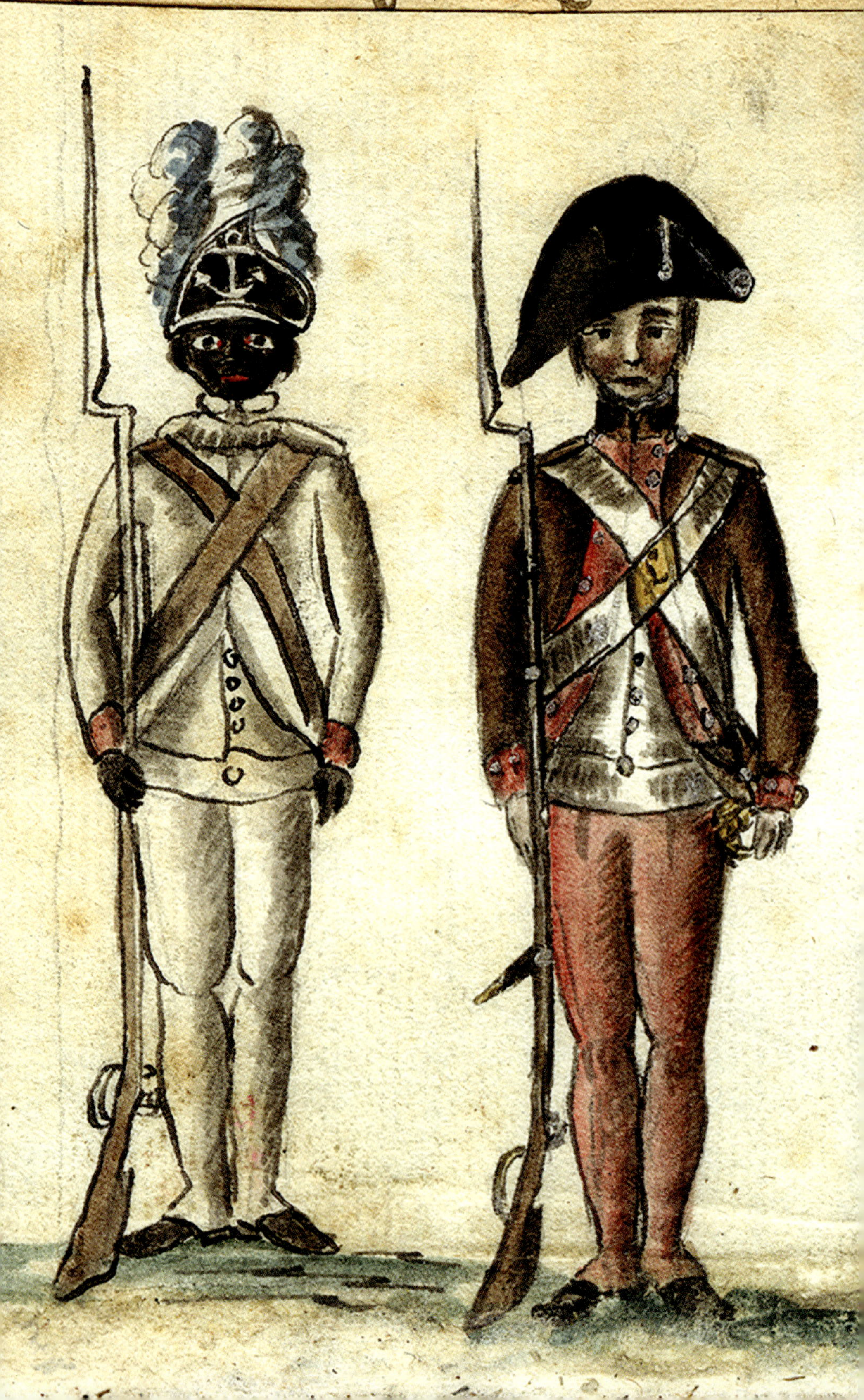

INTRODUCTION

The Minorities Who Fought in the Revolutionary War

Throughout history, soldiers have laid down their lives for their countries. Today, brave men and women pay the ultimate price to defend their nations and to defend their freedoms. Yet **minority** soldiers historically have not experienced the same freedoms or treatment as their white counterparts. This was especially true during the American Revolution. The era preceding, during, and after the war was a time of terrible inequality. African Americans were often treated as property; they were not even considered to be full American citizens. (This book will refer to African Americans by the term nonetheless.) Native Americans lost their land and were treated as outsiders. The struggle of minorities in the Revolutionary period was immense. In the face of violence and inequality, African Americans, Native Americans, and other minorities joined the patriots and took up arms for the

Opposite: This watercolor shows a black soldier from the First Rhode Island Regiment and a white New England militiaman.

American cause. Their valor and contributions to the war effort are often overlooked.

To understand the role of minority soldiers, we must first put the soldiers who fought into context. Among other things, the American Revolution, sometimes called the War of Independence, was influenced by the seemingly unfair rules that Britain's colonial administrators enforced against Americans. The colonial administrators came to America to lead the colonies on behalf of England, just as many Americans had come from England to start a new life free from the religious restrictions that oppressed them in their home country. Events such as the Boston Massacre helped to motivate Americans to join together, take action, and fight for their independence.

Records were not kept as accurately in those days as they are today. However, there was an official government **census** in 1790, shortly after the Revolutionary War ended. This, the first census in the country's history, provides an understanding of the demographics of the new nation. At that time, the land mass of the United States was much less than it is today. There were thirteen original colonies, or states: Connecticut, Delaware, Georgia, Maryland, Massachusetts, New Hampshire, New Jersey, New York, North Carolina, Pennsylvania, Rhode Island, South Carolina, and Virginia. There were also a few other territories (the Southwest Territory, which would later be known as Tennessee; a district called Maine, which was then part of Massachusetts; and the district known as Kentucky, which at that time was part of Virginia). The borders of some of the states and territories were different then than they are today. Much of what is the current United States was at that time owned and controlled by France, Spain, and Russia. The colonies and territories of the United States were, until the Revolutionary War, under colonial rule by England.

According to the 1790 census, there were a total of 3,929,328 people in the United States of America. The census categorized the demographics as follows:

- *Free white males of sixteen years and upward: 813,365, or 21 percent of the population*

- *Free white males under sixteen years: 802,127, or 20 percent of the population*

- *Free white females: 1,556,628, or 40 percent of the population*

- *All other free persons: 59,511, or 1 percent of the population*

- *Slaves: 697,697, or 18 percent of the population*

Different categories were measured for different reasons. Free white males who were sixteen or older, for example, were counted to find out the number of potential workers for industry and the number of people who might participate in the military.

From this census information, it appears that in 1790, 3,172,120 people in the United States were white. This would have been 81 percent of the population at the time. In terms of minorities, they comprised 19 percent of the population, or 757,208 people, at the time.

The census of 1790 measured only a few categories of people, unlike the many categories that were later added.

People who lived in the areas controlled by France, Spain, and Russia—many of them Native Americans and settlers from other places—would not have been counted in this census. Also, because this census was taken after the Revolutionary War, soldiers killed in that war would not have been counted. Native Americans who lived among the general population and followed national and state laws in what had become the United States would have been counted in the "All other free persons" category. On the other hand, Native Americans who lived on tribal lands would not have been counted in the census. Thus, the census of 1790 was not as accurate as modern censuses.

Population measures for people living in the United States colonies, territories, and districts from around 1775 give slightly different numbers:

- *Free whites: 2,100,000, or 74 percent of the population*
- *White indentured servants and convicts (present and former): 50,000, or 2 percent of the population*
- *Native Americans: 200,000, or 7 percent of the population*
- *Black slaves: 500,000, or 17 percent of the population*
- *Total population: 2,850,000*

Of this total, 2,150,000, or 75 percent were white, and 700,000, or 25 percent, were minorities.

These census figures provide a sense of the makeup of the population at the time of the American Revolution. Though it is unlikely that these figures are completely accurate, they give us a broad sense of who was living in the United States during colonial times. More importantly, these figures point to the struggles of both African Americans and Native Americans, who were such a small percentage of the population.

Approximately five thousand African Americans joined the American side to fight in the Revolutionary War. Because approximately three hundred thousand Americans in total joined the fight against the British, this means that fewer than 2 percent of those soldiers were black. But numbers are not everything. It is remarkable to think of the major impact that minorities had on the war in the face of inequality. Over the course of this book, we will trace the achievements of the brave soldiers who helped secure American independence. We will also examine the treatment they received—both fair and unfair—before, during, and after the war.

—SNYDER

ONE

Life at Home

At the advent of the slave trade, each of the thirteen original colonies allowed slavery. During the Revolutionary War, the vast majority of slaves lived life the way they had before the war. In other words, while the war was being fought, most slaves had the same day-to-day existence they did before. They worked in fields of tobacco, cotton, and other crops. They tended livestock. Some served in households as servants. They performed whatever other tasks they had been assigned. Most slave owners would not have allowed their slaves to participate in the war. They did not want to risk losing the free labor, and they considered their slaves to be their property. For these reasons, most African Americans did not fight in the war, and so the war did not substantially change their daily lives.

Opposite: **Slaves, such as this one, were often whipped by slave owners.**

Native Americans, on the other hand, faced different circumstances in the United States. African Americans lived in disparate circumstances based on whether they were free or enslaved. And if enslaved, experiences varied depending on how their masters treated them and what their tasks were. The lives of Native Americans at that time were even less homogenous. Some Native American tribes lived on their own, far away from the European Americans who had come and taken over a good deal of their land. Other Native American tribes lived in harmony, and sometimes in conflict, with white people. Some tribes adopted the white colonists' customs. Furthermore, some tribes became dependent on products of European origins, growing to need items such as firearms. Often, Native American and white communities, along with their African American members, lived alongside each other. They depended on one another. Native Americans who lived close to towns settled by Europeans and their slaves often participated actively in the local life and economy. These Native Americans sold items such as food and firewood in town markets. They worked as servants and laborers to earn money. Some also learned new trades in order to earn a living. In short, it is difficult to generalize about the experiences of minorities—during the Revolutionary era or any other time. Yet there are important facts about the lives of slaves, free African Americans, and Native Americans that shape our view of history.

THE LIVES OF SLAVES AND FREEDMEN

To live in bondage, as slaves did, was to experience unimaginable horrors. Many slaves faced severe mistreatment or abuse at the hands of their masters. If they tried to run away or to disobey their masters, they could be beaten or tortured. At times, slaves were even murdered for these offenses. To make life more difficult, many slaves had been separated from their families when their owners bought them. Their spouses and children may have been sold to different owners than they were. In addition, slaves originated from many different countries in Africa. Therefore, they had different cultures and languages. All of this made it difficult for them to communicate with one another. This, along with the punishment they feared receiving from their masters, broke the spirits of many slaves and put them in a position where obedience to their masters was likely. There were laws in many colonies making it illegal for slaves to run away from their master's farm or plantation, and these laws provided for the forcible return of runaways.

Some African Americans were not enslaved. By 1776, free African Americans made up approximately 8 percent of America's total population of African Americans. In some colonies, these free African Americans had almost the same rights as other free Americans. In other places in America, free African Americans' rights to property ownership and other freedoms were legally restricted. In fact, slavery and racial discrimination were underpinned by the laws of the time.

Some free African Americans had been born free; others became free through lawsuits where they argued for their freedom. Others still bought their freedom or escaped. Free African Americans made a living much as free European Americans who were not wealthy did: they earned money practicing various trades and farming. Free African Americans who did not fight in the Revolutionary War would most likely have lived during the conflict much as they did before it.

THE LIVES OF NATIVE AMERICANS

Native Americans worked in a variety of professions; they were blacksmiths, seamstresses, wood carvers, masons, and potters. In a few documented cases, white people chose to live

This engraving shows John Wesley preaching to Native Americans, many of whom followed religions other than Christianity.

within "Indian" communities instead of living in their own communities. (Note that Native Americans have sometimes been called Indians. When European explorers discovered them in North America, they first mistakenly believed they had reached India instead. Therefore, these explorers called the natives Indians, which is not an accurate description.)

Before the Revolutionary War, many battles between Native Americans and white settlers had been fought. As a result, many entire Indian communities and tribes were wiped out by European settlers. Some natives were killed purposefully or accidentally by diseases, such as smallpox, influenza, bubonic plague, and measles, after these diseases were brought from Europe. Native Americans were not resistant to these new diseases like Europeans often were. Due to escalating conflict and the rapid spread of disease, Native Americans often did not trust European Americans, and European Americans often did not trust Native Americans.

At times, Native American tribes **assimilated** into European culture. However, others retained much of their original culture. Their cultures were very diverse because of the differences between different tribes. Overall, Native Americans were forced to give up many of their cultural practices, adopting European practices in their place. Some Native Americans, for example, converted to Christianity. In fact, many of the Native Americans who ended up fighting in the Revolutionary War were Christians. The Oneida Indians are a good example of widespread assimilation: they lived in large, framed houses, used metal silverware, ate on pewter plates, wore clothing made of flannel, and illuminated their houses with candles. This was unlike other tribes who still lived in the traditional

Virginia settlers from around 1610 building homes on Native American land

Native American ways. Commonly, tribes lived traditionally but adopted a handful of European practices.

On a day-to-day basis, Native Americans (and African Americans) had to fight for their freedom and sometimes their lives as the colonists were fighting for emancipation from Britain. Later, some of these colonists would have to reconcile their values about freedom as they came to see that they, too, were oppressors.

NATIVE AMERICAN CIVIL RIGHTS BATTLES IN THE 1700S

At the time of the American Revolution, there was a prevalent attitude that people of other races were inferior to white people, and this racist attitude included people of mixed races, such as people with mixed white and black, black and Native American, or white and Native American ancestry. Of course, not all white people felt this way. There were various legal and **civil rights** battles that happened both before and during the Revolutionary War. These battles involved seeking better treatment for African Americans and Native Americans.

Close to the revolution, Native Americans from different areas in America, including Georgia and Maine, lodged complaints with colonial authorities about the fact that colonists continued to trespass on and take their land. These land grabs had happened ever since Europeans invaded Native American lands in the Americas, killing and displacing many indigenous people in the process. This time the Native Americans complained about more of their land being taken and about being squeezed off their already reduced territory. They also protested colonists' attempts to fraudulently take their land. Over time, colonists had taken Native American land by tricking them, conning them into agreeing to deals that were not to their advantage, or outright lying. Native Americans warned that if this did not stop, they could not control what their sons would do. Some of their sons had been raised as warriors and were willing to go to war with the colonists who attempted to take their land and possessions. Colonial authorities were unable or unwilling to do much to help Native Americans in these situations. As the Revolutionary War began, however, both patriots and loyalists backed away a bit from trying to take land from Native Americans. Americans and the British sought to repair, at least somewhat, their relationship with Native Americans so they would not be fighting each other and Native Americans at the same time.

Aside from land, another battle for better treatment came from Native American chiefs and other representatives. They were concerned about another problem that Europeans had brought to Native American communities: alcohol. Many Native American chiefs raised objections, without result, to colonial administrators and other legislators about the ill effects that the sale of alcohol, such as rum, brought to their people. Some colonial officials tried to make it more difficult for Native Americans to obtain alcohol. Others did not care or were even happy that alcohol destabilized Native American communities.

ABOLITIONISM

The **abolitionist** movement had begun in the previous century, the 1600s, and it became stronger in the 1700s. There were various proponents of ending slavery, including some religious groups (such as the Quakers) and some political figures of the time. The first anti-slavery publication in America dates back to 1688; "The Germantown Protest" was written by Pennsylvania Quakers who outlined their religious arguments against slavery. They said slavery was wrong and went against their beliefs in the basic human rights that should be provided to all people. Other anti-slavery publications came out later, such as Samuel Sewell's 1770 essay entitled "The Selling of Joseph." Like "The

Germantown Protest," Sewell argued that slavery was evil and said the men who owned slaves were immoral.

Equal Rights Fighters

Thomas Jefferson, who owned slaves, would write in the Declaration of Independence in 1776 that "All men are created equal." One prominent abolitionist from England, Thomas Day, noted the irony of this in 1776. He said, "If there be an object truly ridiculous in nature, it is an American patriot, signing resolutions of independency with the one hand, and with the other brandishing a whip over his affrighted slaves." This quote eloquently points out the discrepancy and hypocrisy in the fact that many of the men behind the Declaration of Independence owned slaves yet proclaimed all men equal. These men did not really believe that liberty, inalienable rights, and equality were concepts that applied to everyone. Most of them probably believed that these rights applied only to free white males. Females, too, at the time were not universally considered equal to men and were often made to live by rules their fathers or husbands set for them. In fact, some colonists grappled with this discrepancy throughout the war.

One of the people who gave voice to the abolitionist movement and the desire of all humans to be free (slaves included) was Phillis Wheatley. Wheatley was born in Africa. In 1761, when she was seven years old, she was transported to America on a slave ship. She was purchased as a slave by the Wheatley family, who lived in Boston, Massachusetts. Her master was Susannah Wheatley, wife of a rich tailor. Phillis was purchased to become part of the household domestic staff. However, she demonstrated great intelligence and the ability

Benjamin Franklin, John Adams, and Thomas Jefferson drafting the Declaration of Independence

to learn extremely quickly. With help from books and from lessons taught by Mrs. Wheatley, Phillis learned how to read and write. These were skills that most slaves never learned. Many slaves were barred from education due to laws that outlawed teaching slaves to read and write. Some slave owners feared that educating slaves would lead to uprisings against them.

Phillis Wheatley was the first black slave in America to become a published poet.

Life at Home 21

At the age of fourteen, Phillis composed her first poem. Her writings, as they developed, often concentrated on the themes of American freedom from Britain and freedom for black slaves, as well as for all people. The people who read and were affected by her poems included George Washington and Voltaire. Wheatley, whose writings helped to encourage the abolitionist movement in America, was the first black slave to write and publish a book of poetry. She was also the third woman in America to publish a poetry book. This book, published in 1773, was called *Poems on Various Subjects, Religious and Moral*. She was granted her freedom after the death of her master in accordance with her master's will.

Wheatley's work has stood the test of time and remains a searing indictment of slavery. In a letter she wrote and published in 1774, Wheatley discusses freedom:

> *The glorious Dispensation of civil and religious Liberty, which are so inseparably united, that there is little or no Enjoyment of one without the other: Otherwise, perhaps, the Israelites had been less solicitous for their Freedom from Egyptian Slavery; I do not say they would have been contented without it, by no Means, for in every human Breast, God has implanted a Principle, which we call Love of Freedom; it is impatient of Oppression, and pants for Deliverance; and by the Leave of our Modern Egyptians I will assert, that the same Principle lives in us.*
>
> *God grant Deliverance in his own way and Time, and get him honor upon all those whose Avarice impels them to countenance and help forward the Calamities*

of their Fellow Creatures. This I desire not for their Hurt, but to convince them of the strange Absurdity of their Conduct whose Words and Actions are so diametrically opposite. How well the Cry for Liberty, and the reverse Disposition for the Exercise of oppressive Power over others agree,—I humbly think it does not require the Penetration of a Philosopher to determine.

Another famous advocate for ending slavery was Thomas Paine. He was one of the people known as the "Founding Fathers" of America. Paine was born in England but moved to America, where he worked as a tailor. In 1776, he published a pamphlet, *The American Crisis*, for which he is most often remembered. It encouraged American rebels to fight against what he considered unfair British rule. He also fought against England. In 1775, however, he had published an article in a Pennsylvania newspaper by the name of "African Slavery in America." In it, Paine argued passionately against men owning slaves. He pointed out how wrong and inhumane it is for people to be enslaved. The first paragraph of this reads, rather poetically:

That some desperate wretches should be willing to steal and enslave men by violence and murder for gain, is rather lamentable than strange. But that many civilized, nay, christianized people should approve, and be concerned in the savage practice, is surprising; and still persist, though it have been so often proved contrary to the light of nature, of every principle of Justice and

African Americans Fighting in the French and Indian War

Often in colonial America, especially before the Revolutionary War, there were policies prohibiting African Americans from serving in armed conflicts. At times, they were not permitted *any* involvement in conflicts, armed or otherwise. At other times, as in Virginia in 1756, African Americans were permitted to serve in the **militia** only as musicians or laborers but not to take up arms.

Dire need changes things. In 1754, a full-scale conflict between France and England in North America erupted. It was an extension of the Seven Years' War between France and England in Europe. This conflict, often called the French and Indian War, involved disputes between France and England over their land borders in North America. Most of the battles were fought by the British army. Sometimes they were supported by colonial militia, and because of the war's severity, some restrictions on African American participation in armed conflict were lifted.

Just as in the Revolutionary War, accurate records were often not kept during the French and Indian War. One record that shows the race of **enlistees** from North Carolina from 1754, under Colonel William Easton, lists seven minority soldiers. Five of them were black. Two of them were of mixed black and white racial heritage. Records from two other companies from the same time period from North Carolina show eight

Painter Henry Alexander Ogden's representation of the Battle of Ticonderoga, a key battle during the Seven Years' War

African American soldiers fighting alongside their European American counterparts. Other colonies, such as New York, Connecticut, and Massachusetts, utilized even more soldiers of African heritage in their units. As in the Revolutionary War, these minority soldiers served their country when it needed them.

Humanity, and even good policy, by a succession of eminent men, and several late publications. Our Traders in MEN (an unnatural commodity!) must know the wickedness of the SLAVE-TRADE, if they attend to reasoning, or the dictates of their own hearts: and such as shun and stiffle all these, wilfully sacrifice Conscience, and the character of integrity to that golden Idol.

There were also many more advocates for the abolition movement. The Reverend Samuel Hopkins was a New Englander and the pastor of the First Congregational Church of Newport, Rhode Island. In 1770, he became increasingly active in the abolitionist movement. He worked to convert

Anthony Benezet lived from 1713 to 1784 and dedicated himself to the abolitionist cause.

his friends and neighbors to the anti-slavery cause. He even went to speak to men who owned slaves. Hopkins explained his position on the immorality of slavery and asked them to free their slaves. He was so convincing that in one instance he was able to persuade one of his friends who owned a slave to free the slave immediately.

Also around 1770, a Quaker schoolmaster named Anthony Benezet vocally opposed slavery for religious reasons. Benezet took several concrete steps to work against slavery. He wrote to leaders in both America and Europe to ask them to support ending slavery. Additionally, he started finding all the anti-slavery material that he could. He reprinted the material and distributed the pamphlets and books. Benezet even started a school in 1770 in Philadelphia to help prepare African American children of free parents for freedom and success. (Pennsylvania abolished slavery in 1780. Many other colonies took even longer to legally eliminate slavery.)

In the next chapter, we will examine the Revolutionary War itself in detail so that we can understand how it unfolded. Then we will look at the experiences of some of the minorities who fought in it.

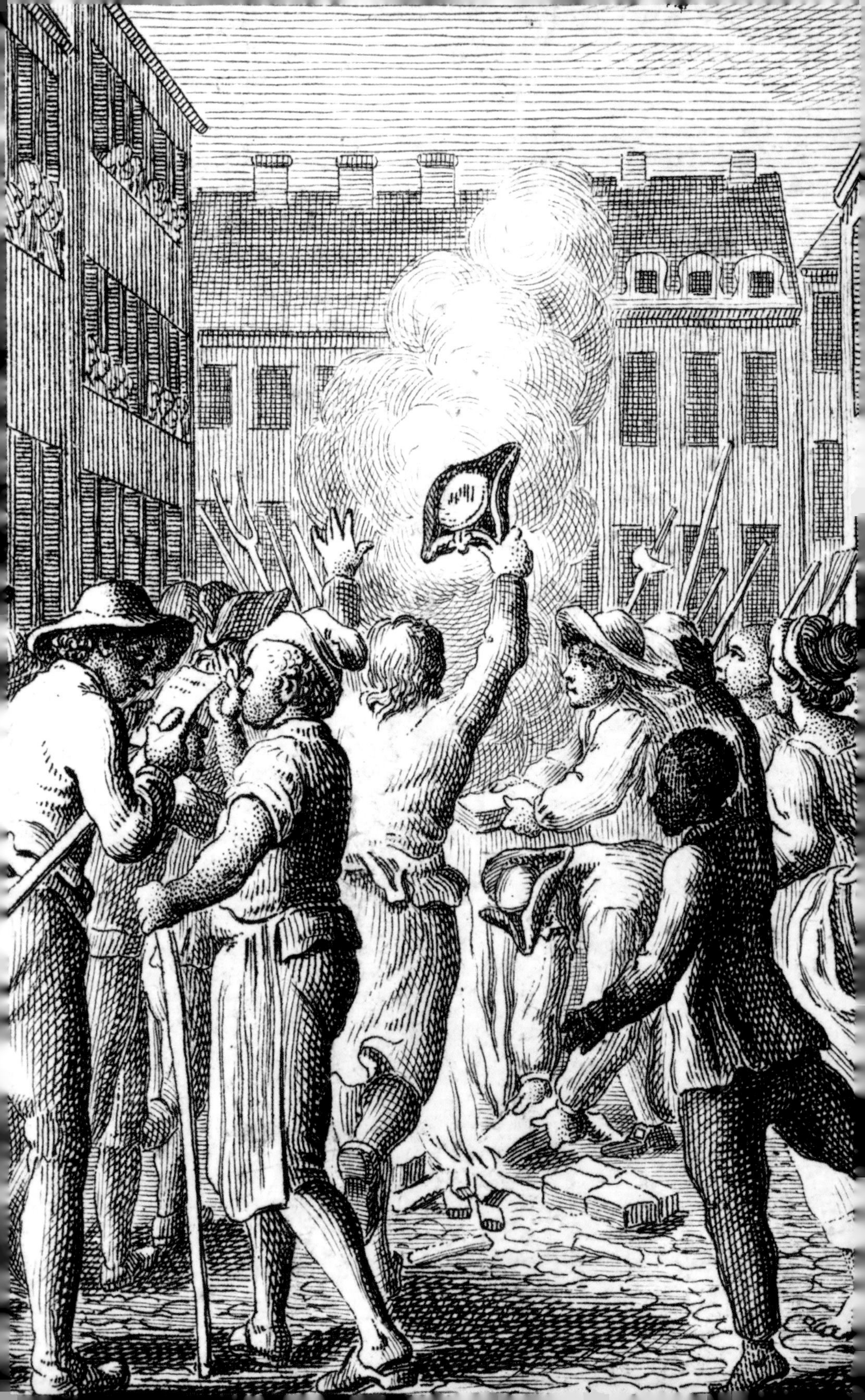

The Revolutionary War Itself

The Revolutionary War officially lasted from April 19, 1775, to September 3, 1783. As with most wars and conflicts, there were legitimate **grievances** against both sides in the Revolutionary War. Colonists wanted more control over their daily lives; they wanted a voice in shaping the laws that affected them. Colonists also became increasingly concerned that England did not have their best interests in mind as the British government enacted new laws and policies that affected colonists' businesses and day-to-day lives. Americans especially did not appreciate being taxed without having representation in the British government.

By 1775, many Americans favored limiting England's power, though the American Revolution was not about securing independence at first. The buildup to war happened gradually and spanned more than ten years. It is noteworthy that the people who originally came to America from England

Opposite: American colonists protesting England's Stamp Act

came to both avoid religious persecution and to have freedom from the British government. They were generally self-reliant and strong-willed people. It is no wonder that they and their ancestors would resist control from the government of England in America.

EVENTS LEADING UP TO THE WAR

Before the American Revolution began, tension had been increasing between the government in Britain and American colonists ruled by Britain. To start, the Sugar **Act** in 1764 gave more power to British **customs** officers. It allowed them to search ships and warehouses for smuggled goods. It also placed increasing restrictions and regulations on basic foreign imports, including sugar, coffee, and wine. Sugar, for example, was often imported from France; Britain wanted to make sure that it was paid taxes on this import. Acts like these did not go over well with colonists in America who were already facing a tough economy and high unemployment.

Then England introduced the Currency Act in 1764, which made the use of paper money in the colonies illegal. (This was an extension of the Currency Act of 1751, a law that applied only to New England.) England figured that colonial manufacturers based in America, who were often paid with paper money, would be driven out of business. The intent of the act was to ensure that colonists instead purchased goods manufactured in England. The Currency Act also tried to prevent colonial smuggling of goods, a common practice that gave colonists access to Dutch, French, and West Indian products.

Another act increasing American resentment toward England was the Stamp Act in 1765. This was the first direct tax that was placed on colonies by England's **Parliament** and the first act that dealt with tax related to domestic trade. The Stamp Act raised money for Britain by requiring the use of the stamp (or watermark), which was just government-issued paper. The stamp was required on certain products and goods or as an additional part of the cost of various services. Most colonists believed that only their local assemblies should be able to tax them directly as the Stamp Act did. The act drastically redefined the colonists' relationship with England, and people were outraged. Colonists who were loyal to England, however, did not protest this new tax. After much protest, the Stamp Act was **repealed** in 1766.

The Townshend Acts were then passed in 1767 and required colonists in America to pay taxes on products made within Britain's empire and sold in America. It taxed such products as paper, paint, glass, and items made of lead. All of these were products that Americans bought from England. In addition, the Townshend Acts put a three-penny tax on tea, which almost all American colonists consumed. Americans protested and chose to **boycott** affected products as much as possible.

The Boston Massacre

The Boston Massacre in 1770 was another event that pushed colonists toward war with England. The Townshend Acts brought about complaints, defiance of British laws, and protests in Massachusetts and other colonies. Many colonists around the country, except for British loyalists, defied the Townshend Acts. This embarrassed both the king and England's Parliament. To reduce protests, England called for more British troops to stand guard in Massachusetts. This was to get control of the people. British troops, customs officials, and other officials had been harassed by Americans protesting the Townshend Acts and other treatment by Britain considered to be unfair.

In October 1768, four thousand British soldiers came to Boston. They made life difficult for locals and tried to take more control of the colonies. Occupation by British soldiers continued somewhat peacefully until 1770. Yet as tensions increased, many people expected that violence would happen as a result of the occupation. On March 5, 1770, a violent confrontation occurred between Americans and British troops who were guarding the customs house in Boston. The protesting Americans threw snowballs that may have contained bricks and rocks at the British troops. As the situation escalated, British troops fired on the crowd, killing five men and wounding eight other American colonists. A free black and Native American sailor named Crispus Attucks and four white laborers were killed. After news spread of the event, Americans became more suspicious that England was trying to deprive them of their rights and freedoms. The British became more convinced that America wanted to continue to rebel more against their control. Later in 1770, the British government repealed the Townshend Acts.

Edmund Burke, a member of Parliament who was sympathetic to American freedom, said this before the Boston Massacre:

> *The Americans have made a discovery, or think they have made one, that we mean to oppress them; we have made a discovery, or think we have made one,*

that they intend to rise in rebellion. We do not know how to advance; they do not know how to retreat.

This quote is an excellent illustration of some of the tensions between England and America.

The Boston Tea Party and the Coercive Acts

The Tea Act was another unpopular measure initiated by the British government in 1773. The Boston Tea Party protested the Tea Act. American colonists also engaged in other defiant acts. England's government was angry at Americans for rebelling. The government of England expected Americans to pay their taxes, as ordered and without resistance or protest. Therefore, it passed a series of further restrictions known as the Intolerable Acts (also called the Coercive Acts). These acts included measures such as closing Boston Harbor until Americans paid for the tea they threw in it during the Boston Tea Party in December of that same year. It gave some of America's land to Canada to decrease its land mass (known as the Quebec Act). It forced Americans to provide housing and supplies for British troops and representatives (known as the Quartering Act, which meant British troops could take over a family's private home if they so chose). It also greatly limited how much locals could assemble and run their own government in Massachusetts. Colonists now needed permission of the British governor of their state for such activities. These new laws were meant to reassert British authority in Massachusetts. What they succeeded in doing, however, was alienating American colonists even more and further dividing colonists who were loyal to the British government from those who favored America having self-rule (called rebels or patriots).

The First Continental Congress

The Continental Congress served as the governing body of the thirteen original American colonies. Then it acted as the government of the United States. The rule of the Continental Congress lasted from 1774 until 1789. The First Continental Congress in 1774 was formed in response to the Coercive Acts. Present were representatives from twelve of the thirteen colonies (there were no representatives from Georgia in attendance). The congress passed resolutions that declared that the Coercive Acts violated colonists' rights. These resolutions said that they would not obey the dictates of the acts. The congress also encouraged the people of Massachusetts to form a government responsible for collecting taxes and holding the money until the acts were repealed. It recommended strong economic **sanctions** against Britain. This congress also advised the people of America to arm themselves and thus form their own militias to protect themselves against the British government. Even at this point, full-scale war with England was only considered a last resort.

MAJOR BATTLES AND EVENTS OF THE WAR

On April 19, 1775, militias engaged in a firefight with British soldiers in Massachusetts in the cities of Lexington and Concord. In this battle, 73 British soldiers were killed and

174 were wounded. The Battles of Lexington and Concord officially began the Revolutionary War.

The Second Continental Congress

In light of the events of the Battles of Lexington and Concord, the congress worked to prepare the colonies for war. It authorized the creation of a Continental Army,

The Revolutionary War started with the Battles of Lexington and Concord.

choosing George Washington to serve as commander. It also authorized American paper money that could be printed to purchase supplies. It appointed a committee to handle foreign relations. Some delegates of this congress still thought that it might be possible to avoid war with England, though. They wrote the Olive Branch Petition, which said that American colonists would end their armed resistance if the king would repeal the Intolerable Acts and withdraw England's military from America. King George III rejected the proposal, sealing the inevitability of war.

American colonists began to understand that peaceful arguments would not settle their numerous and deep differences with England. Armed conflict seemed the only way after all else had failed. Americans had tried measures such as peaceful protest, defiance of Britain's laws that were deemed unfair, and reasoning with British officials in America and England. As the war approached, most people who joined the armed forces did so voluntarily. In some states, draft systems were instated that required able-bodied men to fight. Some people were able to avoid service through deferments for different reasons. In the case of wealthier people, they could pay not to have to serve or send a substitute, such as a slave. In some cases, a poorer citizen would be paid by a richer man to serve in his place.

The Declaration that Changed Everything

The Second Continental Congress, with its delegates representing the colonies, continued to meet, though they had to move their meeting place from Philadelphia to Baltimore during the final months of 1776 in order to avoid being captured by British forces headed toward Philadelphia.

Earlier in 1776, the congress passed the Declaration of Independence, written by Thomas Jefferson. It formally declared their intent to be independent from England and establish their own government.

This historic document begins:

In Congress, July 4, 1776.

The unanimous Declaration of the thirteen united States of America,

When in the Course of human events, it becomes necessary for one people to dissolve the political bands which have connected them with another, and to assume among the powers of the earth, the separate and equal station to which the Laws of Nature and of Nature's God entitle them, a decent respect to the opinions of mankind requires that they should declare the causes which impel them to the separation.

The declaration then explained more about why America was declaring its independence from England. It included a list of over twenty things that England, its legislators, and King George III had done that were considered unreasonable. These included items such as not always allowing Americans a trial by jury, a right that was extended to everyone in England, and the imposition of taxation without representation. American subjects felt they should have had the right to represent themselves and make decisions in Parliament, just as British subjects did.

King George III of England rejected America's Declaration of Independence.

As a result of these offenses and others, the colonists asserted their right to freedom:

We, therefore, the Representatives of the united States of America, in General Congress, Assembled, appealing to the Supreme Judge of the world for the rectitude of our intentions, do, in the Name, and by Authority of the good People of these Colonies, solemnly publish and declare, That these United Colonies are, and of Right ought to be Free and Independent States; that they are Absolved from all Allegiance to the British Crown, and that all political connection between them and the State of Great Britain, is and ought to be totally dissolved; and that as Free and Independent States, they have full Power to levy War, conclude Peace, contract Alliances, establish Commerce, and to do all other Acts and Things which Independent States may of right do. And for the support of this Declaration, with a firm reliance on the protection of divine Providence, we mutually pledge to each other our Lives, our Fortunes and our sacred Honor.

After American officials signed this document, they sent a copy to King George III. He did not accept the declaration; instead, he decreed that Americans were in a state of rebellion and no longer loyal to the crown. He also told his government to prepare for more battles in America. (Note that in 1781, the Continental Congress also **ratified** America's first constitution, known as the Articles of Confederation. This document served as the constitution of the United States until 1789, when the US Constitution that is now in effect was ratified. All of these

★ ★ ★ ★ ★ ★ ★ ★

Bushnell's *Turtle*

Most of the technology that was used in the Revolutionary War was not new and had been around for a while. The weapons employed included **mortars**, **muskets**, and cannons. These had all been used in previous battles and were no surprise. There was, however, one new type of technology that was experimented with and used during the Revolutionary War. This new technology was the submarine. The use of the submarine is arguably the most interesting instance of new technology used in the war. The first submarine designed specifically for warfare was invented in 1775 by a man named David Bushnell. He also fought in the war. The submarine was called the *Turtle*.

Bushnell's *Turtle* was designed to submerge and then direct an explosive at an enemy ship. It was first used in the Revolutionary War on September 7, 1776. Submarines had been around for 150 years at that time (and designs for the vessels trace back to the Middle Ages), yet this was the first time they had been used in naval combat. The submarine was called the *Turtle* because of its resemblance to the reptile. It was designed to be hand powered underwater by one operator. Its specific purpose was to attach a bomb to the hull of enemy ships. The first time that it was used, the submarine failed to properly attach a bomb to a British ship named the HMS *Eagle* in New York harbor. Although the bomb did not attach to ship, it exploded nearby. It injured no one. The explosion may

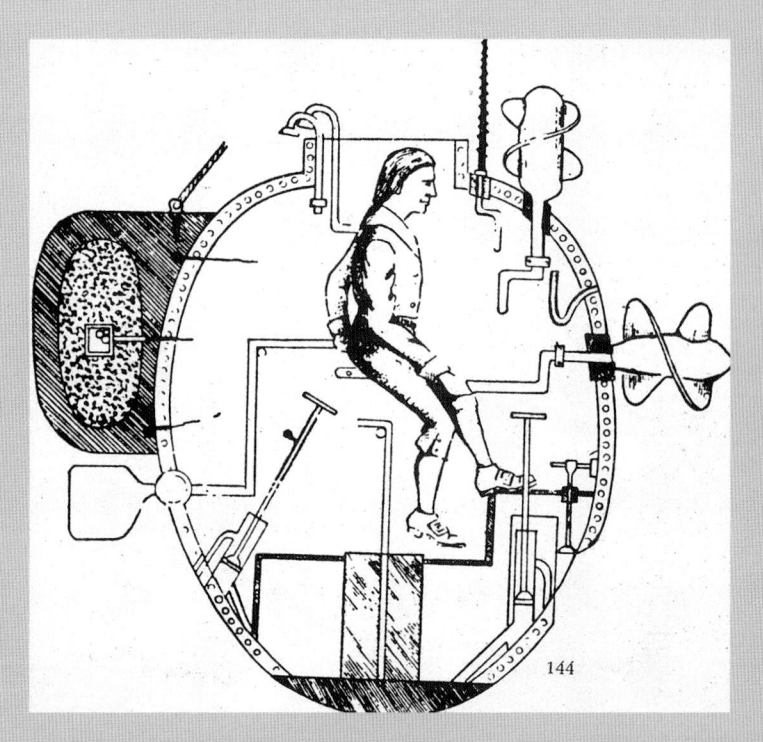

The first submarine designed for use in naval battles was not successful.

have made the British more watchful, however. The *Turtle* never actually successfully sank a British ship in the Revolutionary War. The submarine was lost when the American ship that was transporting it happened to be sunk by the British.

steps were significant in the United States of America becoming its own, self-governing nation.)

The Battle of Saratoga

One turning point in the war was the Battle of Saratoga, which was fought on two different days eighteen days apart. During the first part, on September 19, 1777, British General John Burgoyne led his troops to victory against the Americans. On October 7, 1777, however, there were very different results. On this day, American troops defeated General Burgoyne and his troops, causing them to retreat and him to surrender later. This was a major battle in the American War of Independence. The victory helped Benjamin Franklin secure an alliance with France, and the nation contributed financially as well as with supplies and troops. Historians believe that the Battle of Saratoga gave America the momentum to win the war.

However, many obstacles stood in the way of victory. Between 1779 and 1781, America underwent a number of setbacks and losses in battles in the war, as well as some small victories. This included one of their leading generals, Benedict Arnold, changing loyalties from America to England. (Even today Benedict Arnold's name is synonymous with the word "traitor.") British troops also occupied Georgia. In 1780, they captured Charleston, South Carolina, which was a big loss to Americans because it prevented their access to the port there, cutting the Americans off from manpower and supplies.

The Battle of Yorktown

At the Battle of Yorktown in 1781 in Yorktown, Virginia, American troops under the command of General George

After the Battle of Yorktown was won by the American army, General Charles Cornwallis surrendered to General George Washington.

Washington fought fiercely for several weeks, from September 29 to October 19. British troops suffered heavy losses and captures by American troops, who were assisted by around eight thousand French soldiers. The British realized they were doomed in this battle when they were surrounded by American and French forces by land and sea. The British had underestimated the perseverance of American troops and their allies. England also underestimated the strength of French forces. The British realized they could not sustain their military effort against America. One factor that worked to the advantage of America and to England's disadvantage was the fact that everywhere battles occurred, there were Americans ready to fight for their country.

General Charles Cornwallis was second in command of British troops in America, under his commander, General Henry Clinton. Cornwallis surrendered at Yorktown on October 19, 1781. This effectively ended the war, though the war would not officially end for two more years.

WAR'S END

During the war, American patriots bravely fought British troops (nicknamed "Redcoats" because of the red uniforms they wore). American soldiers were led by General George Washington, who later became the first president of the United States. The troops fought on in the face of incredible hardship, including shortages of food and inadequate clothing. Some fought through harsh winters without shoes, for example. Also, the armed forces were not adequately trained. Despite these shortcomings, General Washington treated his troops well. He worked hard to get them the supplies that they needed whenever possible. Washington led them to victory in several key battles of the Revolutionary War, and so his troops respected his leadership. In turn, Washington appreciated their loyalty and dedication. Remarkably, Washington helped a very young country with an army that was not organized or well-trained beat England's well-trained and organized army—in spite of stacked odds.

After the battle at Yorktown, British forces still fought American troops. Yorktown, however, was the last major battle in the American Revolution. After this, many people in England turned against the war. In 1782, the year after the Battle of

Yorktown, England elected a new Parliament. This Parliament was pro-American, and they voted to end the war. Negotiations for peace began shortly after their vote.

Many loyalists evacuated the United States after the Revolutionary War ended to return to England. During the war, there were many colonists in America who remained loyal to the crown. In 1783, the Treaty of Paris was signed in France between the United States of America and England. It officially ended the war and made America a self-governing nation. As the treaty states, America and England were now willing to "secure to both perpetual peace and harmony."

The first article of the treaty reads:

His Brittanic Majesty acknowledges the said United States, viz., New Hampshire, Massachusetts Bay, Rhode Island and Providence Plantations, Connecticut, New York, New Jersey, Pennsylvania, Maryland, Virginia, North Carolina, South Carolina and Georgia, to be free sovereign and independent states, that he treats with them as such, and for himself, his heirs, and successors, relinquishes all claims to the government, propriety, and territorial rights of the same and every part thereof.

The Treaty of Paris was signed by three Americans, including George Washington and Benjamin Franklin. Now, the British no longer had any claim to govern Americans or own land in the colonies. It also meant that the boundaries of the United States could expand westward across North America if the American government chose to do so. They did, later extending borders all the way across the continent.

A Call for African Americans to Fight for the British

Lord Dunmore, the last colonial governor of Virginia and a British official who was known for causing trouble for American rebels, issued an important proclamation on November 7, 1775. Dunmore's decree offered freedom to slaves and indentured servants willing to escape and fight for the British military. In his proclamation, Dunmore declared **martial law** and called all rebels traitors to the British crown. Although he did not successfully increase the size of the British forces because of this proclamation, he did gain some new recruits. More importantly, Dunmore stoked American patriots' resentment and anger toward the British government. He also increased slave owners' fears of slave rebellions. Dunmore ultimately freed few slaves.

John Murray, known as Lord Dunmore, Virginia's final British governor, offered freedom to slaves who would fight for England.

Lord Dunmore's proclamation was issued on November 7, 1775.

Part of the proclamation emphasizes the consequences of being a traitor to the crown:

> I do require every Person capable of bearing Arms, to [resort] to His MAJESTY'S STANDARD, or be looked upon as Traitors to His MAJESTY'S Crown and Government, and thereby become liable to the Penalty the Law inflicts upon such Offences; such as forfeiture of Life, confiscation of Lands, &c. &c. And I do hereby further declare all indentured Servants, Negroes, or others, (appertaining to Rebels,) free that are able and willing to bear Arms, they joining His MAJESTY'S Troops as soon as may be ....

At the height of the war there were around 133,000 British troops and 96,500 American troops in the Continental Army. Of those British forces, around 13,000 were Native Americans. Around 25,000 slaves and free African Americans fought during the war, representing both sides. Overall, 50,000 or more soldiers died in the Revolutionary War, and there were civilian casualties as well. Though the battles themselves were deadly, more soldiers died of disease, on both sides, than were actually killed in battle. Before modern medicine, this was common in conflicts. American soldiers also faced disease when captured by the British: illness, mistreatment, and bad conditions on British prison ships took their toll. American prisoners of war were three times more likely to die on these prison ships than to die in battle.

EFFECTS OF AMERICA'S VICTORY IN THE REVOLUTIONARY WAR

The Revolutionary War was an important military victory that helped create a long-lasting democracy. It added to and reinforced the sense of independence and self-reliance that many Americans already felt. The Revolutionary War also shaped the world in several ways. First, it decreased England's global dominance. In the colonial era, Britain was trying to take over as much of the world as possible and had succeeded in conquering and ruling various countries and territories on multiple continents. Because of this, it was said that the sun never set on the British Empire. The loss of control of America was a big blow to England's plans. By winning, the United States of America positioned itself to become one of the most powerful countries in the world. Furthermore, the ideals that the colonists fought for, such as freedom and independence, entered public consciousness. These ideals, unfortunately, did not extend to most minorities who lived in America at the time. And it is the tension between these ideals and the reality of life for African Americans and Native Americans that would later forever alter the history of the United States. In the next two chapters, we will examine two examples (among many) of the heroism and bravery demonstrated selflessly by minorities serving during the Revolutionary War. One chapter will describe the unique contributions of a black slave. Then we will look at Native American tribes who helped win freedom for Americans.

This is to Certify that the Bearer by the Name of James Has done Essential Services to Me While I Had the Honour to Command in this State. His Intelligences from the Ennemy's Camps were Industriously Collected and More faithfully deliver He perfectly Acquitted Himself with Some Important Commiss I gave him and Appears to me Entitled to Every Reward his Situation Can Admit of. Done Under My Hand, Richmond November 21st 1784

Lafayette

A Waiter Spying on the British: A Case Study

Throughout history, in order to fight and win wars, armed forces have relied on more than just soldiers, and the Revolutionary War was no different. Without soldiers, wars cannot be fought. But without people serving in other positions, wars cannot be won. People serving in a wide variety of positions are needed in wars, including servants, cooks, medical personnel, and even spies. In many wars, including the American Revolution, spies were used in various ways to gain information and intelligence from enemy forces. This information included what enemies' plans were, when and where they might attack, what weapons and capabilities they had, and other vital pieces of information.

During the Revolutionary War, spies had to collect and send information to their allies verbally. Sometimes spies communicated by writing and sending letters through allies. Instead of hacking computer systems, secretly reading emails,

Opposite: **James Armistead was a slave whose service as a spy during the American Revolution helped to secure his freedom.**

and tapping into phone calls, they had to listen in person to secret conversations. Spies often had to physically steal important documents to help their cause, too. Many African Americans, some of whom were free and some of whom were slaves, served in the Revolutionary War as soldiers. Many other African Americans served as spies, either for the Americans or the British.

This chapter examines the life of one spy who played a vital role in the Revolutionary War: James Armistead. James was an African American slave owned by William Armistead of New Kent County, Virginia. Like many African Americans at the time, James was born into slavery. He grew up on Armistead's plantation. (Slaves in that time sometimes took their master's last name. We will refer to James as James Armistead, as many sources do, even though it is not clear that he ever actually went by the last name of his owner. What we do know is that once he gained his hard-earned freedom, he chose to go by the name of the man who helped him secure his freedom.)

Slave owners often did not keep detailed records of when their slaves gave birth, so James's date of birth is not known exactly. Also, records that were kept during the Revolutionary War were not always as accurate as records and documentation that is kept today. Therefore, some history is based on direct evidence while some is based on available documentation.

It is thought that James Armistead was born around 1748 in New Kent, Virginia. When he was in his early thirties, he wanted to be of service to the American cause in the Revolutionary War. The Americans at that time had sent out requests for able-bodied men to serve in the battle to defeat the British. Therefore, Armistead asked his master's permission to join the Continental Army. William Armistead granted his request. William had an interest in the American side of the revolution; he served as the Virginia state commissary of military supplies. He did not stop James from serving on the American side and was probably happy for him to do so.

JAMES ARMISTEAD, SPY

James Armistead began service under the Continental Army Major General Marquis de Lafayette in March 1781. Lafayette had come from France to Williamsburg, Virginia, to help the American cause and was asked to lead French troops who were serving there. The Marquis de Lafayette was the commander of the French forces allied with the American Continental Army. Lafayette was trying to keep Benedict Arnold from causing more trouble in America, specifically in Virginia. Because Lafayette realized how intelligent and observant Armistead was, he hired him as a spy for the Americans. In addition, Lafayette felt that this slave, who was volunteering his services, would be loyal to the American cause of freedom. There must have been something special and unique about Armistead to make Lafayette put so much trust and faith in him.

To gain the trust of the British, Armistead posed as an escaped slave who wanted to help the British cause. He got a job as a servant to the British, serving Benedict Arnold and his men. Armistead later served Charles Cornwallis, a British army officer and the colonial administrator in the United States.

At the time, Britain was one of the world's greatest superpowers, having conquered countries around the world.

The Marquis de Lafayette commanding American troops at the Battle of Yorktown, assisted by an unknown servant

America had often lost battles in the Revolutionary War, so intelligence gained through spying was vital to their success. It would have been believable to the British leaders and troops in America that James wanted to get away from his life of slavery. Plus, if the British won the war, James would most likely have

54   Minority Soldiers Fighting in the American Revolution

been given his freedom because of his service to them. The British, therefore, had no reason to suspect that he was not a runaway slave and that his loyalties were with the Americans. James was hired.

Espionage behind Enemy Lines

At times, James Armistead served as a forager, gathering food for troops and their leaders in the army. James knew the region where he worked very well and did not need a map to make his way around. All of this helped him to travel without restriction so that he could visit the American camp as needed. After the British grew to trust him, they hired him to spy on the Americans. Because James Armistead was employed by both the British and the Americans to gain information, he was what is referred to as a double-agent. His real loyalties, however, were with the Americans. The British had no idea he was not on their side.

James gave the British fake information designed to hurt them or to thwart their goals. Meanwhile he provided the Americans, including General Lafayette, with valuable information about the British. If he knew, for example, that the Americans planned to attack a certain location, he could tell the British that the Americans had not discussed any plans to attack or say that they had plans to attack somewhere else. He also could have given the British fake information about what weapons and equipment the Americans had. Any fake information he gave the British could have helped to make them make faulty decisions or be less prepared than they were, helping the Americans to win. Yet he had to be careful not to be obvious in providing the British with faulty intelligence so

James, shown here in his later years, was skilled at obtaining secret British information and giving it to America.

that they would continue to trust him. Also, if they had found out he was a double-agent, they may have killed or imprisoned him for it.

Many of Lafayette's troops had been killed in battles led by Cornwallis. Therefore, Lafayette needed very trustworthy information about the movements and plans of enemy British troops to defeat them. When Armistead learned helpful information, he was able to send it back to Lafayette secretly. Armistead put his life in danger by being a spy and gathering secret information to help the Americans.

Benedict Arnold also trusted James Armistead enough that he sometimes asked him to help guide British troops around the local area. This also made it easier to travel freely between the American and British camps. Because the British military officers trusted him, they sometimes discussed their plans and strategies for defeating the Americans right in front of him. Armistead would deliver reports to other spies on the side of America or to Lafayette himself.

Armistead would sometimes go to Lafayette's camp himself to deliver critical information that he had gained from the British through **surreptitiously** spying on them. Often, however, sometimes daily, messengers from Lafayette's camp would secretly meet Lafayette as he was out and get information from him to take back to the Americans. There may have even been other messengers and spies for the Americans who served the British as double-agents and who could also have delivered information for Armistead. We cannot, however, be sure of this. (It is noteworthy that it may have also been possible for Armistead, with the freedom that he had during the war, to escape from service and from slavery altogether, although he did not do this.)

One way that James Armistead helped Lafayette was by repeating to the general the conversations among British military leaders that he overheard while he served as a waiter at the headquarters of General Charles Cornwallis, stationed in Yorktown. He also carried other messages back and forth. He was even able to smuggle papers from General Cornwallis's command center so that General Lafayette would know more about the plans of the British.

Armistead and the Yorktown Campaign

During the summer of 1781, General George Washington requested that General Lafayette provide as much information as possible about the British army's plans and strategies, as well as about the people fighting for them and their equipment.

When Benedict Arnold and his men went farther north, so did Armistead. At that point he was able to get close to General Cornwallis's camp and learn useful details about the plans of the British. James Armistead continued spying for the Americans while acting as a servant at Cornwallis's camp during the Yorktown campaign. He gave information to General Lafayette that sealed the British army's fate at Yorktown.

At one point, it is likely that Armistead learned the British naval fleet was planning to relocate ten thousand soldiers to Yorktown, Virginia, and that they were going to have a central command location there. It seems that Armistead was able to provide Lafayette and George Washington with extremely detailed information about the plans the British had. Washington was surprised that the British were planning to move to Yorktown, but he was happy to have such important strategic information in advance. With the help of both French and American soldiers, a large blockade was formed. This blockade crippled the British military, halted their plans, and was a major reason that they surrendered to the Americans on October 19, 1781. All of this shows how crucial James Armistead's actions were in helping the Americans win the

Cornwallis surrendered to Washington after realizing that the British could not win the war.

Revolutionary War. Without James Armistead's information about the plans of the British troops, it is possible that the Americans may not have won the war.

After Americans defeated the British at the Battle of Yorktown in 1781, General Cornwallis surrendered. Even though some fighting continued for the next couple of years, America had essentially won the Revolutionary War; their freedom from Britain's colonial rule officially ended in 1783.

The Battle of Yorktown was significant for several reasons. It was the battle that signaled to the British that they needed to surrender to the United States. The British learned that they could not keep up the fight against the United States indefinitely. There were rebel Americans willing to fight the British wherever they went throughout the United States. This worked to the disadvantage of the British since their troops were not nearly as widespread as American troops. The Battle of Yorktown ended up being the last major battle during the Revolutionary War.

ARMISTEAD AFTER THE WAR

Though James Armistead fought for the freedom of Americans, he was not given his freedom immediately after the war. Lafayette praised James for his steadfast loyalty, his dedication to the cause of American freedom from British rule, and his help securing the British surrender after the Battle of Yorktown.

Despite this praise, James Armistead returned to his life as a slave after the war. Because he had served as a spy, he was not eligible for his freedom under a 1783 law that freed slaves who had served as American soldiers. When Lafayette came back to America in 1784 and learned that James was still a slave, he wrote a letter about Armistead's exemplary work. The letter was delivered to the state legislature. Armistead himself also petitioned for his freedom. With the approval of the General Assembly of Virginia, Armistead was given his freedom in 1787. As a free man, Armistead adopted the last name Lafayette in honor of the general's efforts to obtain his freedom. He was known as James Armistead Lafayette, or just James Lafayette, for the remainder of his life. After gaining his freedom, he married, had a large family, and made a living by farming in Virginia.

James Lafayette felt, rightfully so, that he was entitled to a military retirement or pension. In 1818, he requested this from the Virginia legislature, and they approved it. Right after his request, he was awarded $60, which was a great deal of money at the time. He was awarded $40 each year thereafter. Just as with his birth, there are few records describing James Lafayette's life after the war. Around 1816, he bought 40 acres (16.2 hectares) of land in Virginia in New Kent County.

It seems that the Marquis de Lafayette never forgot James Armistead's help in winning the war. Years later, in 1824, the Marquis de Lafayette visited Richmond, Virginia. There he saw his former associate in the crowd, called his name, and hugged James, with whom he now shared a last name.

James Lafayette died on August 9, 1830, at the age of approximately eighty-two years old. He demonstrated honor and valor throughout his life, even though he was not given the rights to which he should have been entitled. He worked bravely, risking his life to help secure American freedom. Lafayette is also an excellent example of how someone can fight for their own rights as well as the rights of others, as he was not afraid to ask the government for his freedom or for money to compensate him as a veteran. The fact that Lafayette asked for his freedom and for monetary recognition for his service in the war from lawmakers and officials who were mostly white may not seem like a big deal now. However, in Lafayette's time, it would have been brave and possibly risky for an African American to request the same kind of treatment and rights that were afforded to white people. Lafayette was honorable

James Armistead's Steps toward Freedom

Though few records exist documenting James's life, a few important records have survived. These records include his petition asking the Virginia General Assembly for his freedom. The document, dated November 30, 1786, is composed in the formal style of the era:

> *To the honorable the Speaker & gentlemen of the genl Assembly, ***
>
> *The petition of James (a slave belonging to Will: Armistead of New Kent county) humbly sheweth:*
>
> *That your petitioner perswaded of the just right which all mankind have to Freedom, notwithstanding his own state of bondage, with an honest desire to serve this Country in its defence thereof, did, ... enter into the service of the Marquiss Lafayette: That ... he often at the peril of his life found means to frequent the British Camp, by which means he kept open a channel of the most useful communications to the army of the state: ... he humbly intreats that he may be granted that Freedom, which he flatters himself he has in some degree contributed to establish; & which he hopes always to prove himself worthy of: ...*

The Marquis de Lafayette's letter to the General Assembly on behalf of James Armistead is also a fascinating window into the process of securing James's freedom:

> *This is to certify that the bearer by the name of James has done essential services to me while I had the honour to command in this state. His intelligences from the enemy's camp were industriously collected and faithfully delivered. He perfectly acquitted himself with some important commissions I gave him and appears to me entitled to every reward his situation can admit of. Done under my hand, Richmond,*
>
> *November 21st, 1784.*
>
> *Lafayette*

France's Marquis de Lafayette furthered the cause of equality in the United States.

in both standing up assertively for his own rights and standing up for the rights of his country through his service as a spy. As we will see, not all former slaves were fortunate enough to gain their freedom as Armistead did.

In the following chapter, we will examine the courageous sacrifices that a couple of Native American tribes made during the Revolutionary War when they fought on behalf of Americans. Like Armistead, these Native Americans served without knowing if they would receive the freedom for Americans that would come with victory. Then, in the final chapter, we will discover what life was like for minorities, those who served and those who did not, after the war in the United States.

brave old Hendrick the great SACHEM or Chief of the Mohawk In[dians]
the Six Nations now in Alliance with, & Subject to the King of Great Br[itain]

Oneida and Tuscarora Indians in the War: A Case Study

Many Native Americans tried to remain neutral during the Revolutionary War. At that time, there were hundreds of different tribes in North America. Many spoke different languages and had distinct cultures; Native American tribes waged war with each other from time to time.

Around the year 1205, five nations of Native Americans decided to unite with one another. Each tribe or group considered itself a nation since each one governed itself. Also, each one had somewhat different customs, cultures, traditions, and ways of operating. In this case, however, these separate

Opposite: The Mohawk were part of the Six Nations. Like other members, they had to decide whose side to take in the revolution. A Mohawk chief is pictured here.

nations decided to work collaboratively making decisions for the mutual benefit of all. These groups were the Seneca, the Cayuga, the Onondaga, the Oneida, and the Mohawk. In 1722, the Tuscarora Nation joined the confederation, which was dedicated to peace and cooperation.

The six tribes lived in an area that is today part of the state of New York, though they also conquered many other Indian nations farther afield. At its peak, the confederation controlled areas as far north as Canada, as far south as present-day North and South Carolina, as far west as the Mississippi River, and as far east as to the Atlantic Ocean.

Thanks to their unity and land holdings, the Six Nations (also known as the Iroquois League or the Iroquois **Confederacy**) were the dominant group of Native Americans in the northeast and northwest areas of the modern-day United States. However, everything changed when the first Europeans arrived on the continent. The Europeans claimed land that belonged to the Native Americans, killing many in the process.

With the arrival of Europeans, many Native American tribes lost their traditional ways of life, their languages, and their property. Although most of the consequences of colonization were negative, one change came in the form of a business opportunity: the arrival of Europeans allowed the Six Nations to capitalize on fur trade. The confederation partnered with the Dutch, the British, and sometimes the French. During the French and Indian War in 1755, the Six Nations sided with the British against the French, and the British ultimately won the war. However, once more English settlers came into America, they began taking over land that had belonged to the Six Nations.

To address the violence that had broken out between Native Americans and English settlers, colonial representatives and Six Nations leaders met in 1768. At the meeting, they tried to agree on definite boundary lines and wound up signing what was known as the Boundary Line Treaty. As with many other treaties that were signed and promised to the Native Americans, this one did not last long; English settlers did not stop taking Native American land in spite of the agreement. (Native American history includes many broken treaties and promises from both the United States government and the British government.)

THE SIX NATIONS: NEUTRALITY AND CONFLICT

Before the Revolutionary War, the Six Nations had always remained neutral in American conflicts, for the most part, and worked together as one body. However, they were unable to do so in the Revolutionary War. Some Oneida did support the British, but most supported the Americans. There was division within the Six Nations about which side to support; the American Revolution was a conflict in which brother sometimes killed brother among the Native Americans.

Before and during the American Revolution, both the patriots and the British worked hard to try to gain the favor of Native Americans, including the Six Nations. Because of their encroachment on Native American lands and previous conflicts between them, some Native Americans distrusted the colonists. (Some colonists, on the other hand, also distrusted the Native Americans either because of previous conflicts with them or because they did not understand their customs. This distrust among and mistreatment toward Native Americans existed among both colonists who were American rebels and those who were loyal to the British.) The advantage, in this case, was with the British.

Leaders of Six Nations were concerned about the Revolutionary War as it began and wanted to stay neutral. They did not necessarily understand the reasons why the British were in conflict with their own colonists. The Six Nations considered it a civil war, and it was one that they did not want to be involved in. However, they found themselves unable to be neutral for long. Pressure mounted from both the thirteen colonies and from England. England, for example, tried to insist that the Six Nations Confederacy carry out its obligations as an **ally** of England. Finally, with the Revolutionary War brewing on Six Nations' land, the confederacy found that it was not able to agree on its allegiances. Thus, the different nations and members of the confederacy split, pitting former confederacy members against one another in battle. Sometimes individuals within the same nation had very different opinions about which, if any, side to support. Most of the Six Nations ended up supporting England. They thought that they had more of an opportunity to keep their lands under the British. Also, they remembered their old alliances with England.

On the other hand, the two nations that gave a great deal of support to the American rebel cause were the Oneida and the Tuscarora (a small number of Native Americans from other nations such as the Seneca also gave support to the Americans at times). Supporting the colonists included helping with raids, as well as serving as guides and scouts. The Oneida and Tuscarora nations also supplied the Continental Army with soldiers at times.

Reverend Samuel Kirkland

One reason that the Oneida Indians supported the Americans was the influence of their Christian missionary, Reverend Samuel Kirkland. Kirkland became their missionary in 1776 and spent much time with them, learning a great deal about their lifestyle and immersing himself in it. Kirkland's influence would spread. He served as a counselor and acted as a mediator in their disputes. He also helped to arrange education for Oneida Native Americans. Reverend Kirkland provided them with tools that they would need for farm work and carpentry. He helped poor Oneida people to get the food and clothing that they needed. The Oneida found it hard to believe, as the English told them, that the Americans were evil when people like Kirkland and others had helped them so much. Kirkland's wide influence is one factor that led to the Oneida's support of the American rebels. Other factors that caused the Oneida to side with the Americans against the British were the power that they had lost under the British and the land that the British had taken away from them.

THE ONEIDA AND TUSCARORA NATIONS DURING THE WAR

At the beginning of the war, the Oneida Nation provided their American allies with valuable information; they also helped catch soldiers who had deserted. Members of the Oneida Nation were warriors, spies, and guides for troops. During the war, some Oneida who served as spies were able to **intercept** British communications as well as obtain information about British troops' strategies and movements.

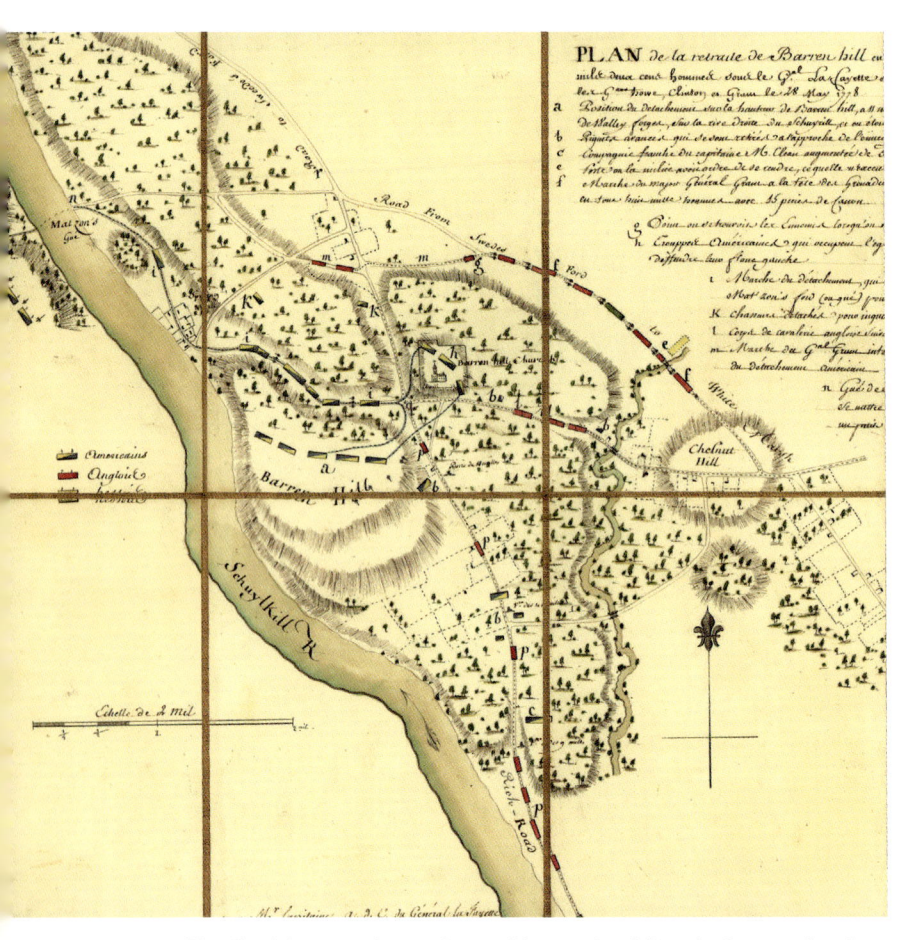

The Oneida served as spies, guides, and soldiers in famous battles. This map shows one such battle.

The Battle of Oriskany

The first battle in which the Oneida fought was an August 1777 battle, the Battle of Oriskany in New York's Mohawk Valley. The Oneida warned American troops in New York on August 2, 1777, that the British were getting ready to attack one of their forts. Four days later, the American militia and the Oneida fought together to defend Fort Schuyler. The Oneida

72   Minority Soldiers Fighting in the American Revolution

and the Americans were able to beat back the British (and the Six Nations Native Americans who were on the British side—the Mohawk). In this battle, which was long and produced many casualties, Native Americans fought against other Native Americans. It was the only battle in the Revolutionary War in which there was such intense combat between members of the Six Nations; this was one of the major battles that determined that the Six Nations would not be united in the American Revolution.

Of course, the Oneida made other contributions as well, providing 150 men to serve as soldiers in 1777 under American General Horatio Gates. This group participated in

Many Native Americans fought bravely on both sides in the Battle of Oriskany.

Oneida and Tuscarora Indians in the War: A Case Study

what became known as the Burgoyne Campaign, including effectively harassing British **sentry**. The Burgoyne Campaign was a series of British attacks named for the architect of the plan, General John Burgoyne. Burgoyne hoped to take control of the northeast, especially a water route between New York and Canada. Gates's defeat of Burgoyne was an important strategic victory, and the Oneida soldiers helped force Burgoyne's surrender.

Washington and Valley Forge

The Oneida and Tuscarora served the Americans under General George Washington's army at Valley Forge, Pennsylvania, during the winter of 1777 and 1778. This was an extremely cold and harsh season. One of the women from the Oneida Nation who went with them served that winter as a cook for Washington.

As previously discussed, the Continental Congress was the official American governing group that helped the different American colonial governments work together to resist British control in the first two years of the American Revolution. It was also known as the Philadelphia Congress. This government tried to balance the needs and interests of the thirteen colonies. It also acted as a **liaison** to England and other nations on behalf of America. As the war went on, this group became the government for the whole nation. In the winter of 1778, the Continental Congress requested four hundred soldiers from their allies from the Six Nations to serve in the American Continental Army. General Lafayette, therefore, asked the Oneida and Tuscarora for volunteers for the army.

Yet the fact that Native Americans fought valiantly for the Americans did not mean they were treated as equals. In a letter George Washington sent to the Commissioners of Indian Affairs on March, 13, 1778, after Congress approved four hundred Oneida for service, he spoke of the Native Americans' "savage customs":

> *You will percieve by the inclosed Copy of a Resolve of Congress that I am empowered to employ a Body of four hundred Indians if they can be procured upon proper Terms 1—Divesting them of the Savage Customs exercised in their Wars against each other, I think they may be made of excellent Use as Sevnts and light Troops mixed with our other parties.*
>
> *I propose to raise about one half the Number among the Southern and the Remainder among the Northern Indians. I have sent Colonel Nathaniel Gist, who is well acquainted with the Cherokees & their Allies to bring as many as he can from thence, 2 and I must depend upon you to employ suitable persons to procure the stipulated Number (about 200) or as near as may be from the Northern Tribes. The Terms made with them should be such as you think we can comply with, and persons well acquainted with their Language, Manners and Customs and who have gained an Influence over them should accompany them. The Oneidas have manifested the strongest Attachment to us throughout this Dispute and I therefore suppose, if any can be procured, they will be most numerous. Their Missionary Mr Kirkland seemed to have an uncommon Ascendency over them and I should therefore be glad to see him accompany them.*

If the Indians can be procured I would chuse to have them here by the opening of the Campaign and therefore they should be engaged as soon as possible, as there is not more Time between this and the Middle of May than will be necessary to settle the Business with them and to march from their Country to the Army.

Aside from the obvious racism of the letter, Washington's request had other problems. Asking for four hundred soldiers from these tribes was a large, unrealistic number. It would have deprived the tribes of a large number of their able-bodied warriors, on whom the nations depended. Their families depended on them also. In a compromise, fifty warriors were provided.

These Oneida and Tuscarora recruits fought at the Battle of Barren Hill in May 1778 under the leadership of General Lafayette. The battle took place in Pennsylvania and involved the Native Americans and other American soldiers attacking the British, engaging them in a short but fierce battle, and securing a British retreat. If the soldiers had not prevented the British from carrying out their plan, almost a fifth of the American army may have ended up captured or killed. Avoiding this trap set by the British was a big win for the Americans and may have changed the course of the war.

The battle saw 2,200 American members of the Continental Army defending Valley Forge and attempting to secure intelligence from British forces. However, the British learned that Lafayette and his soldiers were there and planned to launch a surprise attack on them, hoping to surround and capture them.

George Washington led men, including members of the Oneida and Tuscarora Nations, at Valley Forge, Pennsylvania, in the winter of 1777–1778.

(Lafayette's men numbered around 7,000 to 8,000 in all.) Thanks to his spies, however, Lafayette found out about the British plan on May 19. Therefore, he assigned around 500 regular members of the Continental Army along with 50 or so Oneida and Tuscarora Native Americans with cannons ready to face the British and stop them from progressing. Meanwhile, the remaining troops in Lafayette's group left the area and went to safety. The Native Americans and other soldiers bravely carried out this mission and stopped the British from capturing their men.

Lafayette, the Oneida, and the Tuscarora

Because the Oneida Nation preferred France to England, Lafayette, a Frenchman, was able to recruit them to help against

Native Americans in Conflict

The Revolutionary War brought different nations of the Six Nations into closer contact *and* into conflict. At times, the Oneida engaged in violent conflicts with other tribes from the Six Nations Confederacy, especially those tribes on England's side during the war. The following letter sent to George Clinton, the governor of New York and also a brigadier general in the Continental Army, on Sept. 28, 1778, details the aftermath of one of these attacks:

> *Gentlemen, on Fryday last arrived here the sachems & Warriors of the Oneida & Tuscarora Nations, their number upwards of One hunrd. After the usual formalities, they delivered themselves nearly as follows:*
>
> *Brothers, we have now Taken the hatchet and burnt Unendello & a place called the Butter Nuts; we have brought five Prisoners from each of the above places. Our warriors were Particular that no hurt should be done to Women & Children; we Left four old men Behind who were no more able to go to War … Brothers, we deliver you six Prisoners, with whom you are to act as you Please. Brothers, you had a man scalped here sometime agoe. The Oneidas & Tuscaroras have taken revenge & have brought you some Slaves. We do not take Scalps. We hope you are now convinced of our Friendship towards you & your great Cause.*

the British. Lafayette promised the Oneida that they would serve under French commanders instead of American commanders and be given help building a fort at their settlement in Mohawk Valley, New York. These Oneida and Tuscarora Indians, most of whom had not served in battle for the Americans, were partnered with some of Lafayette's best soldiers, who had been trained extensively the previous winter at Valley Forge by George Washington and other European officers. The success of the Indians and other soldiers at the Battle of Barren Hill restrained the British from causing disaster for American troops.

For the remainder of the war, the Native Americans mainly served the Americans as guides and scouts. They did not see combat, primarily to avoid losing more men, territory, and property than they already had in the conflict. Because of their loyal service, ten soldiers from the Oneida Nation earned commissions as officers in the Continental Army. One was promoted to the rank of lieutenant colonel. As is evident from these examples, the Oneida and Tuscarora served bravely and fiercely in the Revolutionary War, even if there was no definite or concrete advantage to them for helping the American cause of freedom.

SAMUEL MAVERICK
JAMES CALDWELL
SAMUEL GRAY
PATRICK CARR

MARCH 5, 1770.

A Hero's Welcome?

As we have seen, many minority soldiers sacrificed a great deal to end British rule of America. After the Revolutionary War, however, the minorities who fought in the war did not, overall, receive the recognition that they deserved. They had fought for the freedom of Americans, particularly white Americans, yet the minority soldiers (and minority civilians) themselves did not get to enjoy the rights and privileges of freedom. Unequal treatment of minorities was blatantly obvious and even codified into law. Of course, the fight for civil rights for both Native Americans and African Americans continued as well.

TREATMENT OF AFRICAN AMERICANS FOLLOWING THE WAR

The heroic deeds of African Americans who fought on the American side in the Revolutionary War were not recognized

Opposite: This monument honors Crispus Attucks and the four other men who died in the Boston Massacre.

After the American Revolution, the practice of slavery continued until the 1860s.

82   Minority Soldiers Fighting in the American Revolution

partly because there were few written records of their service. Slave owners had denied the vast majority of their slaves a basic education, such as learning to read and write. In fact, it was illegal in many places in America for slaves to be taught to read and write. Because of this, there are few written records by African American slaves about their efforts defending liberty (while denied their own liberty, for the most part). It is unfortunate that many of the heroes of this war have not been widely recognized. While slavery was beginning to be outlawed in some colonies after the war, African Americans still dealt with enslavement, discrimination, and prejudice on a regular basis in the United States. This was also true of Native Americans.

For most African Americans, after the Revolutionary War had ended, life continued as before. Most of those who had fought for the British and been promised their freedom did not receive it. Neither did most slaves who fought on the American side in the revolution. Most of the approximately five thousand African Americans who had fought for America simply went back to the way of life that they had known before, which involved enslavement.

Yet the fight for abolition, which started before the Revolutionary War, continued in various ways until the time of the Civil War. By 1789, many states in the North that had once allowed white people to own slaves had prohibited slavery. Pennsylvania, for example, outlawed slavery in 1780. In the 1860s, all slaves in America were freed, having received their **manumission.**

The Constitution

To examine treatment of Native Americans and African Americans after the war, it is helpful to examine laws that pertained to them. Laws and public policy often give a view into prevailing public attitudes and opinions at the time they are introduced.

The United States ratified the Constitution in 1787. The Constitution includes several clauses that directly affected the lives of slaves. One such clause even says that each African American counts as only three-fifths of a person in the eyes of the law:

> Article I, Section 2, Clause 3
>
> Representatives and direct Taxes shall be apportioned among the several States which may be included within this Union, according to their respective Numbers, which shall be determined by adding to the whole Number of free Persons, including those bound to Service for a Term of Years, and excluding Indians not taxed, three fifths of all other Persons.

This meant that in terms of taxation and numbers of representatives from each state and territory to the two houses of the legislative branch of government, the Senate and the House of Representatives, everyone except for slaves would be counted as a whole person. Slaves would, on the other hand, count as three-fifths. This indicates the inferior status that slaves still had at this time in American history. It reflected the mindset of many, but not all, white Americans at the time. (There were many white Americans who, along with black

Americans, were involved in the abolition movement, on the other hand.)

Another section, Article IV, Section 2, Clause 3, of the Constitution dealing with African Americans is known as the "Fugitive Slave Clause." It states:

> No Person held to Service or Labour in one State, under the Laws thereof, escaping into another, shall, in Consequence of any Law or Regulation therein, be discharged from such Service or Labour, but shall be delivered up on Claim of the Party to whom such Service or Labour may be due.

This clause was a compromise between states where slavery was allowed and states where slavery was prohibited, as indicated in the Northwest **Ordinance** (discussed below). It meant that if a slave who was owned in a slave-owning state escaped to another state, whether slave owning or not, the slave would, if discovered, be brought back to his or her owner and would not, simply by escaping to a state where slaves could not legally be owned, for example, be freed.

The Northwest Ordinance

The Northwest Ordinance of 1797 affected both African Americans and Native Americans. One section that dealt with African Americans prohibited slavery in an area of the United States that was then called the Northwest Territory. This included areas that now make up the present-day states of Illinois, Indiana, Michigan, Minnesota, Ohio, and Wisconsin.

While Article VI of the ordinance was a step toward equality, it also included provisions about the return of runaway slaves:

Article VI. There shall be neither slavery nor involuntary servitude in the said territory, otherwise than in the punishment of crimes whereof the party shall have been duly convicted: Provided, always, That any person escaping into the same, from whom labor or service is lawfully claimed in any one of the original States, such fugitive may be lawfully reclaimed and conveyed to the person claiming his or her labor or service as aforesaid.

George Washington and other founding fathers of the United States ratify the Constitution in 1787

TREATMENT OF NATIVE AMERICANS AFTER THE WAR

The Oneida lost a great deal because of the all-consuming conflict, such as their homes and in many cases their ways of life. They often had few resources after the war. In fact, the Oneida had to wait until 1794, more than ten years after the American Revolution concluded, to be given any **restitution** by the government of the United States. In the end, the Oneida and Tuscarora who had lost property or living quarters because of the war were paid a total of $5,000.

Records do exist of some of the loss claims filed by Native Americans following the war. Here is a claim made by a Six Nations Native American presented to officials of the American government to be compensated for losses of property due to the revolution; it is from the widow of Jacob Anenghrateni:

4 Cows – 2 Horses

1 Sett Horse tackling

1 Sleigh, not shod

3 Large Trunks

1 Chest

12 pewter plates

1 Hand-Saw

2 Large brass kettles

1 small ditto

6 painted Chairs

1 Unfinished framed house with Two Chimneys

1 finished ditto one fire-place

Even though the Native Americans who had fought were compensated somewhat, money could not give them back their culture and ways of life that had been lost. They often found

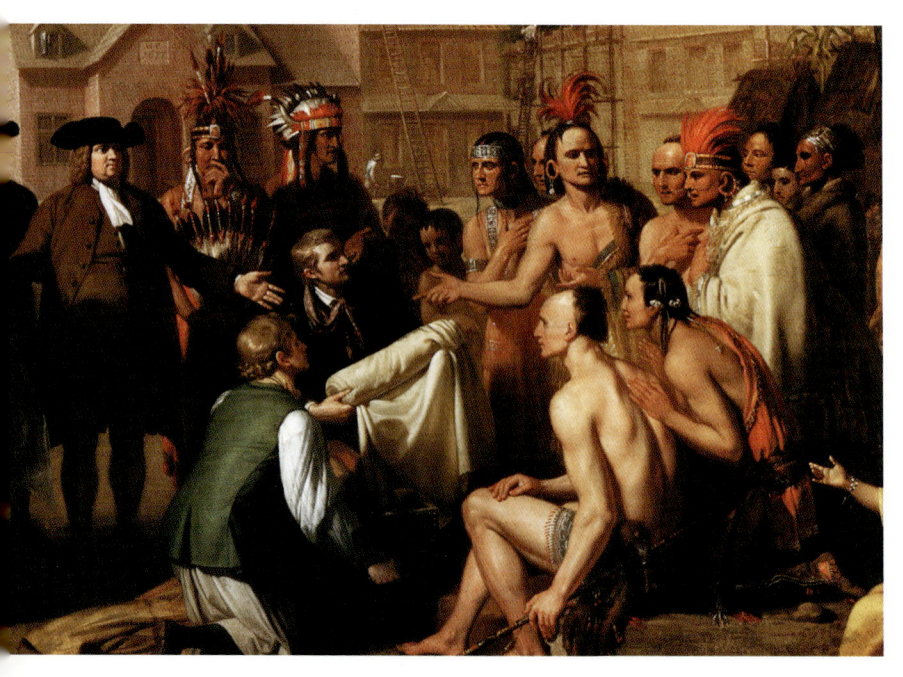

Native Americans tried to negotiate to keep their land—sometimes successfully and sometimes not—with white men.

that they now had to live according to the customs and wishes of the white majority. Also, they continued to lose land, despite various treaties. During the 1800s, some of the Oneida Indians remained on their small area of land in the New York area. Other groups of Oneida Indians, however, moved west to present-day Wisconsin and north to land bought in Ontario, Canada. Long-term division and negative feelings were created between those Oneida who stayed and those who left. Were it not for settlers taking their land and other property and the Revolutionary War, this division within the Oneida Nation may not have happened.

The Northwest Ordinance and the Treaty of Canandaigua

Two sections of the Northwest Ordinance dealing with Native Americans that are particularly interesting to consider in contrast to the Treaty of Canandaigua are discussed below:

> Section 8. For the prevention of crimes and injuries, the laws to be adopted or made shall have force in all parts of the district, and for the execution of process, criminal and civil, the governor shall make proper divisions thereof; and he shall proceed from time to time as circumstances may require, to lay out the parts of the district in which the Indian titles shall have been extinguished, into counties and townships, subject, however, to such alterations as may thereafter be made by the legislature.
>
> Article III. Religion, morality, and knowledge, being necessary to good government and the happiness of

mankind, schools and the means of education shall forever be encouraged. The utmost good faith shall always be observed towards the Indians; their lands and property shall never be taken from them without their consent; and, in their property, rights, and liberty, they shall never be invaded or disturbed, unless in just and lawful wars authorized by Congress; but laws founded in justice and humanity, shall from time to time be made for preventing wrongs being done to them, and for preserving peace and friendship with them.

The two contrasting sections of the Northwest Ordinance effectively made the assumption that what was good for white people was also good for Native Americans. They stated that as America needed more territory, Native Americans would continue to move westward and out of the way, and that the Native Americans could be paid small amounts of money in exchange for their land. After this ordinance was passed, there were several battles between Native Americans and European Americans. And after one of these battles killed over eight hundred American soldiers, President George Washington sent army members to defeat the "problem" Native Americans so that the United States could continue its expansion into the area.

Here are portions of the Canandaigua Treaty of 1794 between the United States government and the Six Nations tribes of Native Americans:

November 11, 1794

The President of the United States having determined to hold a conference with the Six Nations of Indians, for the purpose of removing from their minds all causes of complaint, and establishing a firm and permanent friendship with them; and Timothy Pickering being appointed sole agent for that purpose; and the agent having met and conferred with the Sachems, Chiefs and Warriors of the Six Nations, in a general council: Now in order to accomplish the good design of this conference, the parties have agreed on the following articles, which, when ratified by the President, with the advice and consent of the Senate of the United States, shall be binding on them and the Six Nations.

Article I. *Peace and friendship are hereby firmly established, and shall be perpetual, between the United States and the Six Nations.*

In addition to the first article, the exact land that was to belong to the Six Nations was outlined. Article II then explained that the United States would not in the future try to claim the land belonging to the Six Nations (unless the Native Americans decided to sell and/or America wanted to buy). It referred to their lands as "**reservations**," a concept still in effect for Native Americans today. Article III detailed what land belonged to these Native American groups. The intent of Article IV was that the Six Nations Indians would not try at any point in the future to claim any other land belonging to the United States. (The Six Nations were not given the option of buying more land from the US government.) Article VI then allotted the Six Nations with $10,000 in addition to other compensation. This treaty was signed on November 11, 1794, by fifty Native American officials representing the Six Nations. It was then ratified on January 21, 1795, by George Washington, who was by that time the first president of the United States. The treaty is officially still in place today. It has been upheld some through the years, but parts of it have also been violated. The significance of both of these treaties is that while they provided some benefits to the Six Nations, they accorded far more rights and benefits to the United States of America.

Unfortunately, the Native Americans were once again essentially lied to by the United States, through these treaties and others. Though George Washington upheld the Canandaigua Treaty, it was later broken as white men took more and more of the Native Americans' land due to wars and, significantly, due to westward expansion of the United States. More of their land was taken and their rights were decreased, for example, by the time Andrew Jackson became president in the 1820s. In time, many Native Americans were forced onto reservations or, in some cases, killed as the United States expanded. The equality that white Americans enjoyed did not apply to many Native Americans.

In terms of westward expansion, here is what Thomas Jefferson, a Founding Father and author of the Declaration of Independence, wrote about Native Americans:

> *I have heard with much concern of the many murders committed by the Indians ... in the neighborhood of Pittsburg[h]. Hostilities so extensive [indicate] ... a formidable Combination of that kind of enemy. Propositions have been made for...stations of men as present a safeguard to the Frontiers, but I own they do not appear to me adequate to the object; all experience*

has proved that you cannot be defended from the savages but by carrying the war home to themselves and striking decisive blows. It is therefore my opinion that instead of putting our Frontier Inhabitants under that fallacious idea of security, an expedition must be instantly undertaken into the Indian County.

It might be premature to speak of terms of peace but if events will justify it, the only condition with the Shawnees should be their removal beyond the Mississippi or the [Great] Lakes, and with the other tribes whatever may most effectually secure their observation of the treaty. We have been too diverted by interests of Humanity from enforcing good behavior by severe punishment. Savages are to be curbed by fear only; We are not in a condition to repeat expensive expeditions against them. The business will more be done so as not to have to repeat it again and that instead of making peace on their Application you will only make it after such as shall be felt and remembered by them as long as they a nation.

As is evident from these lines, Jefferson, who also owned slaves and did not believe in them having freedom either, did not consider Native Americans equal to whites. Like many other men of European origin, he defined the Native Americans as savages who were a problem to get rid of. He considered the appropriate way to expand the United States of America westward was to either kill or move the Native Americans who he seemed to believe were in the way.

PERCEPTIONS OF MINORITIES AFTER THE WAR

In the days of the Revolutionary War and beyond, soldiers who returned from war were usually expected to blend back into society and resume their everyday lives. We now know that soldiers returning home from battle need more care for their physical and mental wounds than they received then. Mental health care, for example, would not have been readily available to most soldiers returning from the Revolutionary War; this was not an issue that would even be explored in-depth until modern times. While returning soldiers would have surely been praised for their service, they would have tried to pick up their lives where they left them before the war, aside from receiving military pensions and similar benefits. Unfortunately, it is also true that many heroes of the American Revolution were forgotten about. A great many of the minority soldiers who fought, in particular, were not recognized sufficiently for their service and heroism.

RECOGNITION AND HONORS FOR MINORITIES FOR THEIR SERVICE

Many Native Americans and African Americans who fought in the Revolutionary War were never recognized nor honored for their service. One exception, among a few others, is Jordan Freeman, an African American soldier who was recognized after his death for his service in the Revolutionary War. Freeman had been a slave in Connecticut but was later voluntarily freed by his owner, Colonel William Ledyard, with whom he became friends.

In 1781, the Battle of Groton Heights took place near New London, Connecticut. In this battle, 185 Americans, both

This plaque honors Jordan Freeman and other men fighting in the Battle of Groton Heights.

white and black, tried to defend themselves and their country from 1,700 British soldiers. These soldiers were commanded by Benedict Arnold, who was formerly on the American side but by then had changed sides to fight for the British. In this battle, both Freeman and Ledyard were killed, along with many other

A Hero's Welcome? 95

★ ★ ★ ★ ★ ★ ★ ★ ★

Remembering the First Minority Casualty of the Revolution

The first person killed on the American side of the conflict was a man of mixed African and Native American heritage named Crispus Attucks. Colonists considered him the first

The Boston Massacre turned many Americans against British rule.

casualty of what would become the American Revolution, though the war had not yet officially begun. Attucks was killed, along with four white people, while protesting against British troops on March 5, 1770. The event would come to be called the Boston Massacre, and it occurred five years before the full outbreak of the war.

Two of the white people who were killed were seventeen-year-old civilian boys who just happened to be nearby. Alternatively, people have debated about whether Attucks was a hero or an instigator. The fight began between Americans, including Attucks, and a lone British soldier. After it escalated, a group of British soldiers fired on the crowd. This massacre highlighted tensions that had been increasing between Americans and the British troops. The popular image of the Boston Massacre helped to cement the idea of the British as savage enemies in the minds of many colonial Americans. Later, to honor Attucks, a "Crispus Attucks Day" was celebrated regularly by black abolitionists, starting in 1858. In 1888, the Boston Massacre / Crispus Attucks Monument was placed in downtown Boston.

Native Americans put their lives on the line for the American cause.

Americans. In 1830, the Groton Monument, which recognized the service of all Americans killed, was completed. This is one instance in which an African American fighting for America in the revolution was given recognition for his bravery.

Many minorities fought bravely and selflessly in the American Revolution. Despite the great sacrifices that they made, many of them did not receive the respect and recognition that they deserved nor did they get the benefit of the freedom they fought for or the rights that they should have been entitled to simply for being human beings. Because they were of a different race they were, unfortunately, treated differently.

LOOKING BACK AND LOOKING AHEAD

We have examined what life was like for minorities who lived during the time of the American War of Independence, including those who fought in it. According to the approximate census numbers of people in the United States around the time of the Revolutionary War, it seems that minorities made up less than 20 percent of the total population. Racist ideas and institutions, especially slavery, made life in the new nation difficult for minorities—and sometimes deadly. In spite of inequality and hardship, minority soldiers played a key role in the American Revolution. People like James Armistead Lafayette worked in alternative capacities, too, to help the war effort. Lafayette's role as a spy provided the patriots with intelligence that shaped major battles in the war. Members of Native American tribes like the Oneida and Tuscarora also put their lives on the line for the American cause.

Historically, minority involvement in the Revolutionary War has not been widely discussed. Native Americans and African Americans were discriminated against in the early United States, even though Jefferson wrote about everyone being created equal. The absolute bravery and heroism that minorities who fought in the Revolutionary War displayed should be celebrated and admired. Since their courageous deeds have not always been remembered or honored as they should have, it is important to do so, just as the sacrifices of all soldiers who fought in the Revolutionary War should be recognized, minority and white. Much progress, an admirable and extraordinary amount, has been made since the Revolutionary War in making the United States a land of equality for all. As with most things, there is still even more progress to be made. However, we have moved much closer to a land where everyone is indeed created equal.

Glossary

abolitionist A person who works toward abolishing, or formally putting an end to something, such as slavery or the death penalty.

act A law, statute, or regulation formally passed by a governing body, such as the United States Congress.

ally A nation or state associated with another nation or state, sometimes by treaty, working together as partners toward common goals.

assimilated Having absorbed or adopted the culture of another population or group of people, often in order to fit in with them.

boycott To engage in organized and purposeful refusal to buy from, deal with, or support as a show of disapproval or to try to force certain conditions.

census An official survey or count of a population, often conducted on a regular basis.

civil rights The rights to freedom (socially and politically) and equality to which all citizens are entitled under the United States Constitution and various laws.

confederacy An alliance between two or more parties for the purposes of obtaining common goals or mutual support.

customs Tolls and fees imposed by a country, by law, on imports and/or exports.

enlistees People who sign up or register for service in armed forces, sometimes for a set period of time.

grievances Complaints against another party expressing unhappiness with their unfair and/or illegal treatment.

intercept To catch or stop something from happening, such as a spy seizing a document.

liaison A representative sharing communication between two or more groups, sometimes for the purposes of cooperation and mutual understanding.

manumission The process or act of manumitting, or freeing slaves from enslavement.

martial law Law applied by military occupation or a military government in which ordinary rights and laws are suspended.

militia A group of citizens organized to make a military force, either to add to the regular military or to rebel against the government.

minority A group of people different in some way, such as religion or race, from the larger population group in a specific place.

mortars Any of several types of firing devices used as weapons, such as cannons.

muskets Heavy shoulder guns that soldiers in Revolutionary War times carried.

ordinance A law or regulation set forth by a ruling or governing body, often by a local government.

parliament The highest or the supreme legislative body that governs in a nation.

ratified To be formally approved and confirmed, such as an amendment to a country's constitution.

repealed Rescinded or taken away, canceled by legal authority.

reservations Public plots of land set aside for a certain purpose, such as for Native Americans in the United States.

restitution Payment given in order to try to make up for past injustices or wrongs and to set things right.

sanctions Restrictions, such as punishments or losses of rewards, meant to enforce laws or to punish another entity, such as a foreign country.

sentry A soldier who stands guard over a point of passage, such as a gate or the entrance to a fort or command post.

surreptitiously Done sneakily or stealthily so as to avoid detection, such as a spy listening in on a conversation.

Bibliography

Baym, Nina, ed. *The Norton Anthology of American Literature: Shorter Seventh Edition.* New York: W.W. Norton, 2008.

Berkin, Carol, Christopher Miller, Robert Cherny, and James Gormly. *Making America: A History of the United States.* 6th ed. Vol. 1. Boston, MA: Cengage, 2012.

Carson, Cary, ed. *Becoming Americans: Our Struggle to Be Both Free and Equal.* Williamsburg, VA: Colonial Williamsburg, 2004.

Davis, Kenneth. *Don't Know Much About History: Everything You Need to Know About American History But Never Learned.* New York: Avon Books, 1995.

Dunkerly, Robert. "Overview of the American Revolutionary War: Forging a Nation." Campaign 1776. 2014. http://www.campaign1776.org/revolutionary-war/rev-war-overview/.

Gray, Madison. "James Armistead, Patriot Spy." *Time*, January 12, 2007. http://www.content.time.com/time/specials/packages/article/0,28804,1963424_1963480,00.html.

Graymont, Barbara. *The Iroquois in the American Revolution.* Syracuse, NY: Syracuse University Press, 1972.

Hickman, Kennedy. "American Revolution 101: An Introduction to the Revolutionary War." About Education. 2016. http://militaryhistory.about.com/od/americanrevolution/tp/americanrevolution101.

Higginbotham, Don. *The War of American Independence: Military Attitudes, Policies, and Practice, 1763–1789.* Bloomington, IN: Indiana University Press, 1971.

History.com Staff. "World's First Submarine Attack." The History Channel. 2009. http://www.history.com/this-day-in-history/worlds-first-submarine-attack.

Lanning, Michael. *Defenders of Liberty: African Americans in the Revolutionary War.* New York: Citadel, 2000.

Morris, Richard. *Encyclopedia of American History.* New York: Harper & Brothers, 1953.

National Geographic. *1000 Events That Shaped the World.* Washington, DC: National Geographic, 2008.

Quarles, Benjamin. *The Negro in the American Revolution.* New York: Norton, 1973.

Rakove, Jack. *Revolutionaries: A New History of the Invention of America.* Boston: Houghton Mifflin Harcourt, 2010.

Sawyer, William. "The Six Nations Confederacy During the American Revolution." National Park Service. Retrieved October 5, 2016. https://www.nps.gov/fost/learn/historyculture/the-six-nations-confederacy-during-the-american-revolution.htm.

Sellers, Charles, and Henry May. *A Synopsis of American History*. Chicago: Rand McNally, 1969.

Smith, Alejandra. "Oneida." *The Digital Encyclopedia of George Washington*. Retrieved October 5, 2016. http://www.mountvernon.org/digital-encyclopedia/article/oneida.

Tuchman, Barbara. *The First Salute: A View of the American Revolution*. New York: Alfred A. Knopf, 1988.

Tunis, Edwin. *Frontier Living*. Cleveland, OH: World Publishing Company, 1961.

United States Census Bureau. "1790 Overview." Retrieved October 2, 2016. http://www.census.gov/history/www/through_the_decades/overview/1790.html.

Van Loon, Hendrik. *The Story of Mankind*. New York: Garden City Publishing, 1938.

Further Information

Books

Calloway, Colin. *The American Revolution in Indian Country: Crisis and Diversity in Native American Communities.* New York: Cambridge, 1995.

Davis, Burke. *Black Heroes of the American Revolution.* Orlando, FL: Harcourt, 1992.

Hawke, David. *Everyday Life in Early America.* New York, Harper, 2003.

Phillips, Kevin. *1775: A Good Year for Revolution.* New York, Viking, 2012.

Websites

The American Revolution
http://www.theamericanrevolution.org/

This website is dedicated to the Revolutionary War and includes documents, videos, and information about important figures in the conflict.

History: American Revolution

http://www.history.com/topics/american-revolution

The History Channel's website on the American Revolution contains a wide variety of information, such as videos and articles and a "Digging Deeper" section to gain more in-depth understanding of Revolutionary War history.

Timeline: War for Independence

http://faculty.washington.edu/qtaylor/a_us_history/am_rev_timeline.htm

This website provides an extremely detailed timeline on the Revolutionary War, including day-by-day events and significant occurrences.

Videos

"Meet the First Submarine Used in Combat"

https://www.youtube.com/watch?v=hZTqDjMwejo

This video explains how the *Turtle* was operated and how it was used, unsuccessfully, during the Revolutionary War.

"Who Won the American Revolution? CrashCourse US History #7"

https://www.youtube.com/watch?v=3EiSymRrKI4
Historian John Green provides a quick and humorous summary of the war. The video features context about the time before and after the American Revolution.

Further Information   107

Index

Page numbers in **boldface** are illustrations. Entries in **boldface** are glossary terms.

abolitionist, 18–19, 22, 26, 97

act, 30–31, 33

African Americans, 5, 9, 11–13, 16–17, 24–25, 27, 46, 48–49, 52, 61, 81, 83–85, 94, 98–99

alcohol, 18

ally, 70

Armistead (Lafayette), James, 52–53, 55–63, **56**, 65, 99

Arnold, Benedict, 42, 53, 57–58, 95

assimilated, 15

Attucks, Crispus, 32, 96–97

Barren Hill, Battle of, 76, 79

blockade, 58

Boston Massacre, 6, 31–32, 96, 97

Boston Tea Party, 33

Boundary Line Treaty, 69

boycott, 31

Burgoyne Campaign, 74

Burgoyne, General John, 74

Burke, Edmund, 32

Canandaigua, Treaty of, 89–90, 92

Cayuga, 68

census, 6–9, 98

civil rights, 17, 81

Clinton, General Henry, 44

Clinton, George, 78

colonial administrators, 6, 18, 53

Commissioners of Indian Affairs, 75

confederacy, 68, 70, 78

Constitution, United States, 39, 84–85

Continental Army, 35, 48, 53, 70, 74, 76–79

Cornwallis, General Charles, 44, 53, 56–59

Day, Thomas, 19

Declaration of Independence, 19, 37, 92

demographics, 6–7

diseases, 15, 48

double-agent, 55–57

Dunmore, Lord, 46–47, **46**

education, 21, 71, 83, 90

enlistees, 24

equality, 19, 86, 92, 99

First Continental Congress, 34

Fort Schuyler, 72

Franklin, Benjamin, **20**, 42, 45

freedom, 5, 13, 16, 22, 27, 30, 32, 39, 46, 49, 52–53, 55, 57, 59–63, 65, 79, 81, 83, 93, 96

Freeman, Jordan, 94–95

French and Indian War, 24, 68

Fugitive Slave Clause, 85

Gates, General Horatio, 73–74

George III, King, 36–37, **38**, 39

grievances, 29

Groton Heights, Battle of, 94

Groton Monument, 98

guides, 70–71, 79

inequality, 5, 9, 99

intercept, 71

Iroquois Confederacy, 68

Index **109**

Jefferson, Thomas, 19, **20**, 37, 92–93, 99

Kirkland, Reverend Samuel, 71, 75

Lafayette, Major General Marquis de, 53, **54**, 55–58, 60–63, **64**, 74, 76–77, 79, 99

Ledyard, Colonel William, 94–95

liaison, 74

manumission, 83

martial, 46

mental health care, 94

militia, 24, 34, 72

minority, 5–6, 24–25, 81, 94, 96, 99

Mohawk, 68, 73

Mohawk Valley, 72, 79

mortars, 40

muskets, 40

Native Americans, 5, 8–9, 12, 14–18, 32, 48–49, 65, 67–71, 73–79, 81, 83–85, 87–94, 96, 99

Northwest Ordinance, 85, 89

Northwest Territory, 85

Oneida, 15, 68–79, 87, 89, 99

Onondaga, 68

ordinance, 85–86, 89–90

Oriskany, Battle of, 72

Paine, Thomas, 23

Paris, Treaty of, 45

parliament, 31–32, 37, 45

pensions, 61, 94

Quakers, 18, 27

racism, 17, 76, 99

ratified, 39, 84, 91–92

recognition, 61, 81, 94, 98

repealed, 31–32, 34

reservations, 91–92

restitution, 87

sanctions, 34

Saratoga, Battle of, 42

savages, 23, 75, 93, 97

scouts, 70, 79

Second Continental Congress, 35–36

Seneca, 68, 70

sentry, 74

Six Nations, 68–70, 73–74, 78, 87, 90–92

slaves, 7–8, 11–13, 19, 21–23, 27, 46–48, 52, 60, 64, 78, 83–86, 93

spies, 51–52, 57, 71, 77

submarine, 40–41

surreptitiously, 57

taxes, 30–31, 33–34, 84

three-fifths, 84

Townshend Acts, 31–32

trespass, 17

trust, 15, 53, 55–57

Tuscarora, 68, 70–71, 74, 76–79, 87, 99

Valley Forge, Pennsylvania, 74, 76, 79

Virginia General Assembly, 62–63

Washington, George, 22, 36, 43–45, 58, **59**, 74–76, 77, 79, **86**, 90, 92

Wheatley, Phillis, 19, 21–22, **21**

Yorktown, Battle of, 43–45, **43**, 58–60

About the Author

Eric Reeder is a writer, editor, and proofreader. Reeder has published articles on various subjects, as well as a booklet about different types of editors. He has also written and edited various educational materials over the last sixteen years. In his spare time, Reeder enjoys spending time with his family, swimming, going to the beach, and collecting antiques.